THE UPPER DARBY
POLTERGEIST

THE UPPER DARBY
POLTERGEIST

MARK ALLAN KEYES

Rowe Publishing

ISBN 13: 978-1-64446-007-8

3 5 7 9 8 6 4 2

Printed in the United States of America
Published by

Rowe Publishing

www.rowepub.com

Dedication

There are people that come into our lives that have the ability to impact us in many significant ways, including becoming better ourselves for just knowing them. Virginiarose Centrillo is one of those people. I have had the honor of knowing Virginia for over a decade. She is the primary psychic medium for the PPA and, during that time, she has become a mentor, a teacher, a spiritual advisor, a paranormal partner, and most importantly, my friend. She has selflessly given her time and talent to the service of helping the living cope with the dead, and the dead cope with their passing. This book is dedicated to Virginiarose for touching so many lives and to her husband Chris for sacrificing their personal time together to enable us to work. There are not enough pages a book could contain to express the collective gratitude our team has for Virginia so, I will leave it this way — You are endlessly loved!

Introduction

The pursuit of knowledge and understanding has always been at the core of every paranormal investigation in which I have ever been involved. The Pennsylvania Paranormal Association (The PPA) was created in November of 2007 for the purpose of investigating and resolving claims of paranormal activity for people who were uncomfortable with ghostly activity and wanted it stopped. After spending two years with a local paranormal team in which my wife Lauren and I had the pleasure of being involved, we decided to leave that group to assemble a team of professionals that would focus on identifying the cause of paranormal activity, identify the individual who was haunting the property, if that was the case, and to uncover the intent behind the type of activity that was occurring. Once it was established why the paranormal activity, or haunting, started in the first place, and the intent behind the activity, if any, we could work on a game plan for resolving the haunting, and, hopefully, bring the situation to a happy conclusion.

I am a retired criminal investigator, having worked twenty-five years with the Pennsylvania State Police, and I have a background in psychology. Since becoming a paranormal investigator, I have been involved in more than 200 resolution cases as of this writing. Because of that background, I have always placed as much attention on the victims of hauntings and the way those witnesses perceive events and react to them as I do on the paranormal events themselves. From interviewing people involved, listening to their experiences, and then working through many paranormal investigations, I have learned that people occasionally misperceive events as having a paranormal or supernatural cause, when in fact, a completely normal cause exists behind the activity. The cause may not be standing out to them, mainly because of preprogrammed beliefs from what they have previously seen or heard somewhere in their past. I have also learned that many people who have had an emotionally or psychologically impactful experience with a ghost or have witnessed severe paranormal activity will often lump every weird, out-of-the-ordinary experience into one big ball of *HAUNTED* and profess "The ghost did it!" no matter what the cause. I call this *The Ghost Effect*, which happens when someone becomes fixated on watching for paranormal events to occur because of one profound experience or many smaller experiences over time. Furthermore, without considering other possibilities which may be normal, they may assume that every mysterious event is caused by a ghost. For people who are easily frightened, these experiences force their imaginations to run wild and make matters worse. So, when The PPA investigates, one of our goals strives to separate the normal from the paranormal. At least if an unbiased investigator can find normal causes for some of the activity, especially when those events happen again, the witnesses can relax somewhat, knowing that it was probably NOT a ghost that caused the particular event to happen. Much of what we deal with while conducting our investigations is to look at witness perceptions and beliefs and how people apply those beliefs to what they are experiencing. But what happens when we cannot find logical answers for activity? We then rely on invaluable resources such as our credible, highly-developed psychic mediums with the ability to gather insights into the cause of the reported activity, who may be causing it, and even why. Many teams do not like to use psychic mediums and therefore conduct more "scientific" based investigations. In this manner, they will use a variety of equipment to measure physical changes in the environment or gather evidence on a video or audio recorder. They then investigate to uncover what caused those changes or simply conclude that a ghost was behind the activity because they now have physical evidence to support it. Some investigators even gather names of suspected ghosts through various technical equipment, but that doesn't give much information on why the ghosts are there, how they died, what their intention involves, or if they even know that they are dead. Just gathering physical evidence alone certainly can't remove a ghost from a property. I have worked with and studied several psychic mediums before investigating reported haunted locations, and I can say with great devotion that The PPA is incredibly fortunate to have found an amazingly skilled psychic medium named Virginiarose Centrillo. Virginia has become an invaluable part of our team as a medium, but she is also extremely skilled at debunking activity that does not have a paranormal cause as well as identifying activity that consists of a supernatural nature. Much of the information that we utilized to prepare for and work through the Upper Darby investigation was based on Virginia's insights. By taking a comprehensive approach and analyzing different aspects of events taking place, including Virginia's insights, we were able to establish a reasonable conclusion as to what was taking place there and why.

There are times in life when certain people profess to have a "once in a lifetime" experience, and on occasion these special experiences occur when investigating the paranormal. One location might stand out above the rest, and investigators can only hope to find more locations that consist of such activity as THE ONE. From the viewpoint of a paranormal investigator, the more physical activity on an investigation the better. Physical activity is what we are searching for, waiting patiently for, but on many cases, we don't get to experience what we are looking for. Unlike TV, paranormal investigations are typically quiet. Cases full of activity are an investigator's dream, but it all comes down to perception, who's doing the perceiving, and how they are reacting to it. The most important thing to remember when working for frightened clients is that your amazing experience is likely their nightmare! All due diligence must go into making sure the clients come first and that they are safe. Being an investigator for over a decade and interested in experiencing activity, this haunting turned out to be and still is THE ONE for me. I have never again been part of a haunting where so many people experienced so much, nor have I been able to document so much supporting activity on any other case. When I first spoke with the clients, although I believed most of what they were saying, I thought they were exaggerating levels of activity they had witnessed. It seemed too much, too often, compared to all the previous cases I've been involved with as an investigator. But was I ever wrong for doubting them! If I was dubious in the beginning, I certainly lost those concerns by the end. If nothing else was gained from the events that took place over three investigations adding up to more than a year in time, our team learned an abundance of information and gained invaluable experience. We also became friends with a wonderful family and continue to remain in touch more than nine years later. I can hardly believe that time has so quickly passed, but I am grateful for the experiences and for the people who I experienced it with. Although this would end up being one of our most relentless cases, the family was more than gracious through the entire journey.

Chapter 1

The Request

On March 5th, 2010 at 10:47 p.m., I received an email from a woman named Sharan. The request came through The PPA's online investigation request form. I always take note when a request comes in late at night, because when I follow-up with clients, I often discover that an event has just occurred at their property. Usually, the clients have hit their breaking point, prompting them to reach out for help, and this seemed to be the case!

Because our team at the time was involved with *The Haunted*, a TV series on Animal Planet, one of our initial steps involved carefully reading over the investigation request form to verify the authenticity. Because it was an online form and the show had drawn attention to our site, we sometimes received extraordinarily interesting but invalid request form submissions. I noticed, initially, that the requestor had heard about our team through the television show. However, she had also conducted internet research, which was somewhat reassuring. One of the show's positive benefits for our team is that it made people aware of who we were and that we were available. Many sincere people who did need help could easily find us. After reading through additional information on the form, nothing of concern caught my attention.

As I combed through the request form, I learned that the home requiring attention was in Upper Darby, Pennsylvania, a western suburb of Philadelphia in Delaware County. Upper Darby is a densely populated area with thousands of residential properties. This would make a difference in our physical investigation as we would encounter more abounding noise contamination than in a rural community. The home was listed as a three-story twin-home with three bedrooms and a basement. Because the home was a half-double style house, we would also have to account for any noise that the neighbors were making. Sharan's family consisted of Sharan, her husband, their five children, and a cat. Sharan indicated that the activity had been occurring at their home for three years, and they had lived there for five years. When I learn of cases where activity starts after a family has quietly lived at a location for a considerable period, I take special interest as there is usually a reason for the activity's inception. You will later learn, I was correct. Sharan reported that the activity occurred daily, throughout the day and night. She also reported that other people outside the home had witnessed the activity as well. This was important because a collective line of thinking often exists within a group of people who reside together. Many times, I have found that when more than one person starts to have experiences, the "Ghost Effect" kicks in and propels the haunting to the next level. When people within the same dwelling share their ghostly stories, the number of "events" collectively increases, even if the events are not all paranormal. Grouped together, the occupants then report having a bustling, active location. In the case of Upper Darby, people outside the home who came to visit would also encounter paranormal experiences, which helped confirm these events being likely more than collective misperception.

Going into every case, one of our group's major concerns focuses on whether anyone is being harmed or feels threatened from the activity, especially if it involves children. Sharan felt her son was a target for a portion of the activity. Within his bedroom, Sharan found her son's ball caps formed into a circle on the floor with a toy figurine in the center. The figurine had a drumstick through its neck. Even more troublesome, her son was also being scratched and having items thrown at him. As a parent, I can empathize with her bewilderment, fear, and distress. As an investigator, I must wait and see if we can uncover the intent behind the entire course of conduct and then attempt to determine the intent behind individual events like the ring of hats. Until then, an objective approach must be taken, and each reported event must be individually observed. Additionally, Sharan indicated that she was not aware of any deaths that had occurred on the property.

When deciding on whether a case fits our criteria and later preparing for an investigation, one important area on our request form is the "General Description of Activity." The requestor's activity report helps us decide whether we are going to do a comprehensive physical investigation with all our technical equipment or just a limited investigation with handheld equipment. In some cases, a technical investigation may not be appropriate, and we work with a limited amount of equipment while Virginia utilizes her psychic talent. Sometimes a client reports more psychic phenomena, and other times physical activity is key. Many clients couldn't care less about a physical investigation or documenting activity; they just want to rid their home of the unwanted "guest." In those situations, we do a quick "identify and resolve" type of investigation with only psychic impressions and no equipment at all. In the Upper Darby case, thorough, comprehensive work would definitely be required. Sharan was reporting such a variety of activity that we did not want to miss our chance to document potential activity while we worked. Additionally, I would also learn that while the family was out of the home, somebody or "something" was "trashing rooms" all over the house. In her investigation request, Sharon also reported that the family heard footsteps in various rooms, found items placed behind doors, blocking them from easily being opened, observed lights and children's toys turning on by themselves, discovered the contents of their refrigerator thrown on the floor, watched a ceiling fan (with no power connected) suddenly turn on by itself, found items neatly stacked in different rooms, witnessed an unplugged music keyboard (with illuminated keys) begin to play by itself, found chairs stacked on top of their dining room table, and most daunting, their sleeping baby was moved from one room to another and covered in a blanket from head to toe. This was only a portion of the activity being reported. I could not wait to hear what else was happening. Even the neighbors said they witnessed lights turning on inside the house when no one was home, along with seeing shadows moving about the place. Part of me wanted to go specifically to debunk most of these claims, but if they were all true, the rest of me wanted to document the abundant activity that was taking place.

From the very beginning, this case stood out from all other investigations. Some events seemed fantastical, but the majority were typical yet more numerous than usual. If the reports were all true, and happening daily, I understand why the family reached out for help. Scared for their children's safety, Sharan asked us to contact her immediately. In response to the question, "What do you hope to gain from an investigation?" Sharan answered, "PEACE OF MIND AND SANITY. WE ARE VERY SCARED AND WE WANT ANSWERS." Quite often, clients report feeling as if they are losing their minds. Things are happening that their logical minds can't compute; therefore, fear and panic set in. Most parents have a certain level of concern for the safety and well-being of their children before themselves. When they don't know who or what is causing the activity, and they don't understand why a particular type of activity is occurring, many people feel like targeted victims. It is frightening to think that you can't protect your children because you don't know how, or that an entity may lash out if you do try to protect them. Because this family was reporting extreme activity and because there were five children living in the home, we felt the urgency to make this case a priority. Our quick response was critical. There were no reports of any physical injuries up to this point, and we wanted the situation to remain this way. Emotionally, time would tell how much damage was already done in that respect!

Sharan's online PPA Investigation Request form (see pages 11-12) that gathers basic information to help investigators get a basic understanding of what may be going on at a home or business. (Note: Some personal information has been removed.)

INVESTIGATION REQUEST

Reference #: 5623073
Status: Complete
Date: 2010-03-05 22:47:12
User: [hidden]

First Name: Sharan
Last Name: [hidden]
Street Address: [hidden]
City & State: Upper Darby, PA 19082
Investigation Address or 'Same': same
Phone Number: [hidden]
Email Address: [hidden]

ACTIVITY DATA

How long have you been at this location?
5 years

How long has activity been occurring there?
3 years

Frequency of Activity (monthly, weekly, sporadic):
Daily

Time of day activity occurs the most?
All day and night

Any witnesses other than residents or employees?
YES

General description of activity (i.e., hearing voices, seeing shadows/apparitions, etc.):
Chairs on table, hearing waking noises, blocking doorways, turning lights on, playing with children's toys, trashing rooms, emptying refrigerator contents, very cold attic and lots of activity in attic. Sleeping child was moved from one room to another while sleeping and covered with blanket from head

Page 2 of Sharan's online form:

---

to toe. Neatly stacking of articles, neighbor seeing lights on in home and shadows when we were not home. Lights are often on along with ceiling fans (with no power to them). An unplugged music keyboard with visible moving lit keys and moving of mattress to block entrances. This is only some of the activity that we are dealing with. Please contact us as soon as possible, because we are actually scared for our children's wellbeing. PLEASE HELP!!!

ADDITIONAL INFORMATION

List any deaths at this location. Include name and cause if known:
NOT KNOWN

Has anyone felt threatened or been harmed from the activity? Please explain.
Yes in my son's room with his belongings, the ghost neatly formed a circle with my son's hats and toy figurine in the center of circle and a drumstick through the figurine's neck.

Name and age of all occupants:
2 adults and 5 children

List all pets at this location:
cat

Provide a general description of the location (i.e., 2 story, 3 bedroom house built in 1905 or approx age):
Twin home 3 story, 3 bedroom and basement

What do you hope to gain from an investigation?
PEACE OF MIND AND SANITY, WE ARE VERY SCARED AND WE WANT ANSWERS

How did you hear about The PPA?
Internet and television

Chapter 2

The Interview

After The PPA receives and reviews an investigation request, the next step in our process focuses on reaching out to the requestor by phone and gathering additional information, discussing the situation in more detail, and answering initial questions. We want our clients to thoroughly understand how we conduct our investigations, and we also want to make sure that our team is a right fit with the belief that we can accomplish a satisfactory investigation for the clients. This was certainly the type of case that we would accept, and I was confident that we could help find answers for them. Hopefully we could ease their minds and bring peace back into their home. After all, a home is supposed to be your safe place, your place of comfort, not the place where nightmares are made.

Within a day or two, I reached out to Sharan by phone, one of the steps that I personally enjoy the most. Unlike receiving and reading an email, talking to a client helps me analyze how the person is responding to the activity being reported. The amount of tension in the voice and eagerness to have an investigation conducted can often give insight into the amount of urgency that we, as a team, need to apply to any particular request. Sharan certainly made it clear in her online request that she needed help as soon as possible but speaking directly with her helped confirm that what she was saying matched what she was feeling.

During our conversation, Sharan made it clear that, although she and her husband Gus were not comfortable with the activity, her first priority was her children and that her main concern in reaching out to The PPA was to protect their kids, keep them safe, and halt the activity. I asked Sharan to walk me through the timeline of events from moving into the house until now. She did not remember one significant event that could have started the activity, initially, but we often find that an increase in activity usually begins with turmoil in a family. I questioned if anything stressful had occurred before the initial activity. Sharan explained that the family was experiencing financial hardship. With five kids in the house ranging from an infant to teens, stressful situations were always unfolding. Sharan also mentioned occasional tension with their teenage son at times, but this is a normal occurrence in most families. From our perspective, that was not a huge concern but something we certainly needed to look at later.

A thought I had, when considering the ages of the children in the house was, because several preteen and teenage kids lived in the home, some of the activity, if not all, could be caused by a phenomenon known as psychokinesis. Defined by Wikipedia, psychokinesis is an alleged psychic ability allowing a person to influence a physical system without physical interaction. In more common terms, during a unique child's physical and emotional development, certain "mental energies" build up within the child and are released into the environment without the child's control. In most cases, the child is unaware that this is happening, or that they are the cause for the activity. Psychokinesis often occurs when the involved child undergoes a certain amount of stress, and physical manifestations occur in a home. Light bulbs burst, items are thrown across a room, and slammed doors may even occur. Some poltergeist situations can be traced to a child experiencing these energetic changes.

Sharan had purchased the home, and she and her kids initially moved in by themselves. She was dating Gus at the time, but he didn't move in until later. Sharan relayed that the activity started occurring slowly. The first weird experience happened when she returned home one morning, while the kids were in school, and found a pile of items, originally leaning against the basement walls, pushed together in the middle of the room. Sharan thought her son had moved the items, but when she later asked him, he had not moved anything. Sharan would often find items out of place or moved from a specific place where she remembers having set them. Sharan recalled a conversation with her 80-year-old neighbor, who resided on the right-side of the twin-home, before she had completely moved in. She was moving things in day by day but stayed at her old house until all items had been moved to the new address. During one of the visits to the new house, the neighbor commented that he had seen Sharan there the night before. Sharan asked him what he meant; he told her he saw the lights on with someone moving inside, so he figured she was there. Sharan had not been in the house that night but didn't connect the incident with a haunting until much later when she began suspecting that something unnatural was developing.

Sharan told me that she and Gus eventually married, and Gus moved into the house. But before that happened, she would often call Gus to come over because she was hearing strange noises. There would be knocks and bangs coming from the attic, and she heard footsteps like someone was moving around the house! Gus later told me that he kept thinking Sharan was nuts, but after he moved in, he started to experience some strange things as well.

After being in the home for a couple of years, with small things occurring only now and then, Sharan said she and Gus decided to fix up the house and put it up for sale, not because of the activity, but because they wanted something that better suited their family. In hindsight, Sharan remembers when they started working on their house, Gus tore out an old cubby on the wall of the staircase to the second floor. Immediately after, according to Sharan, this is when activity really picked up.

Historically, people who live in haunted homes for long periods of times often report an increase in activity when they begin doing demolition or reconstruction to the house. This type of occurrence is repeatedly reported to investigators and seems to "jumpstart" more noticeable activity.

Sharan stated that after they began working on their home, many more paranormal events started taking place, and on a much more extreme level. Quite often they would come downstairs and find their dining room chairs stacked on the table. Sometimes the chairs would have tablecloths, previously lying on the table, set on top of them. Items from the kitchen, like jars or dishes, were often found on the table. Most of this activity would occur overnight while they were sleeping. Sharan said they would come downstairs in the morning and always find something new. It was not uncommon to find the kitchen cabinet doors wide open or the drawers pulled out. Sometimes, they would find items from the drawers or cabinets on the floor, and other times, food would be pulled out of the refrigerator and also scattered about the floor.

One of the most frightening and disturbing occurrences happened with the baby. The kids had left for school, and the baby was sleeping in her bassinet located in the master bedroom. Sharan asked Gus to go upstairs and check on the baby, and when he looked, she was not in her bassinet. Gus yelled down to Sharan asking where the baby was sleeping. Sharan answered, "In her bassinet." Gus responded that she was not there. Sharan panicked and ran upstairs where they could not find the baby. They looked in every room on the second floor and couldn't find her, but passing their son's bedroom a second time, they found the baby lying on the bed, completely covered from head to toe with a blanket.

I asked Sharan about the keyboard that was reported to be playing on its own. She told me that they heard noise in the attic and went to investigate. When they got to the room, the keyboard was playing, the lights on the keys illuminated, and the musical tones could be heard. The crazy part? The keyboard was not plugged in. Sharan told me that similar activity had happened in other parts of the house as well. A ceiling fan that was not connected to the electrical power began to spin on its own. A stereo system not plugged in turned on and began to play music, and many of their kids' toys, in different rooms of the house, would often turn on by themselves.

Items were found scattered on the floor, along with the keyboard playing music and lighting up when not plugged in.

Next, I asked Sharan about the circle of hats found in her son's room. Sharan told me that her son had a large collection of hats. One day, she went into her son's room only to find the hats laid out in a circle on the floor, a figurine in the middle of the circle with a drumstick through its neck. Sharon was concerned that her son may be a target and what she saw looked threatening. He complained about seeing a dark shadow going back and forth from the closet to the hallway, and on occasion his arms appeared to have scratches. Once, they found his door closed and had a hard time pushing it open. When they finally did, a pile of clothes and other items from around his room were piled up against the door on the inside, as if someone were trying to barricade it. Sharan and Gus also found another room completely trashed with items thrown all over while in another room they found items such as books, cans, and other objects neatly stacked.

One of the first major incidents happened before they suspected any ghostly activity. One night, the family arrived home to find the house ransacked. Items were thrown all over the living and dining rooms. The kitchen cabinets and drawers were open, and items were pulled off shelves. Sharan said the rooms upstairs appeared as if someone had been looking through them. First, they thought someone had broken into the house and were going to call the police, but they soon realized that nothing had been taken and that all the doors and windows were still locked. After events began to occur on a more frequent basis, they suspected a connection to the haunting.

Sharan sent pictures of the after-effects from these activities, including a picture of the keyboard playing by itself. When first observing the pictures, my initial impressions were that someone really seemed aggravated for some reason. I again wondered if this all could have a little bit of a human cause to it as well. Maybe some of the activity was paranormal but was someone in the house also blaming their actions on a ghost too? These questions arise when I am initially scrutinizing activity in a home. Years later, Sharan told me that I angered her when we first spoke. I asked a myriad of questions which caused her to think I doubted her. Because of the nature of my questions, Sharan was worried that we would not be of help to them. But after working with us for so long, she now understood the method to my madness — looking at events from a criminal investigator's perspective and questioning everything.

When Sharan told me how my questions had affected her, I felt horrible, but in the end, however, I still feel that this approach is much more helpful and honest to everyone involved. If we can find natural causes for activity occurring, we readily point them out. If our methods authenticate reported activity based on a paranormal cause, client reports are confirmed, thereby strengthening their credibility. I have since become more keenly aware of my conversations with people when first speaking with them. On a positive note, after our lengthy conversation I completely believed Sharan's sincerity and honesty and I was looking forward to working with the family.

Sharan talked about countless ghostly encounters during our phone call, but that information would fill a book of its own. I recently encouraged Gus and Sharan to write down their experiences and share their story to help other people who might be experiencing similar events. What will be presented in this writing are the experiences that my team and I encountered as we investigated what would later be known as the Upper Darby poltergeist.

Just one of the many occasions where the family walked into the kitchen to find the cabinets and drawers opened up.

The family returned one afternoon and found a mess in the front attic room.

Chapter 3
Initial Insights

On Friday, March 30, 2010, at 6:15 p.m., The PPA arrived at the Upper Darby home to begin the most physically active investigation which I have ever been involved in. The complete investigation occurred over the course of an entire year with three separate physical investigations and a vast amount of work behind the scenes. The crazy part? Not one of those investigations was more exceptional than the other, but they were all exceptional in their own way!

The assigned team for this investigation comprised of Virginia, our psychic medium, two investigators, Paul and Bob, and I, the director and case manager. The drive to Upper Darby was nearly two and a half hours from our home office, just outside of Scranton, Pennsylvania. During the drive, Paul, Bob, and I had various conversations regarding the upcoming investigation, previous investigations, and various life events that we all were experiencing. Something we always try to avoid, while discussing upcoming investigations, however, is anticipating what might happen. Once you start anticipating an outcome, one way or another, you lose objectivity. We try to approach every case with an open mind and objective outlook, then analyze events as they surface.

With this investigation, I was anxious to either debunk claims or validate activity, whatever way the investigation led us. Either way, I was totally intrigued by the family's claims.

We arrived in the neighborhood where Sharan and Gus lived, turned on to their street, and observed a typical residential area of most city suburbs. Neighboring houses crowded close to each other on both sides of the street. A mild, cloudy evening, near fifty degrees Fahrenheit, bore some humidity but luckily withheld rain. An exciting factor not planned, but a lucky twist of fate, revealed a full moon on this particular evening. Some people believe a full moon can increase the amount of paranormal activity at a haunted site, and we were eager to test this theory. Sunset would soon be approaching, so I wanted to tour the home before dark. Pulling up to the twin-house, I could see inside the well-lit left side that was bustling with activity where Sharan and Gus resided. By activity, I mean living human activity! The upper outside façade was distinctly different than the right side of the twin-structure, giving each side its individual look. The building was three stories tall with windows on each floor. The left side had beige colored siding, and the right was plain white with a large stone chimney dividing the two down the center. The right side of the twin-home was dark inside with only the third-floor attic light illuminating the single window on the front of the house. It appeared that no one was home. We confirmed that the neighbors were away, which would make investigating the right side much easier. When an investigation is conducted with connecting dwellings, a certain amount of noise contamination can make it more difficult to record for sound anomalies. Eliminating noise contamination was a huge bonus. I wondered at the time if the people living on that side of the building were having issues themselves. None were reported to us through Sharan, but it's also possible that the neighbors might have withheld that information.

Before we stepped out of the van, I received a phone call from our psychic medium, Virginiarose Centrillo — Virginia or Ginger, for short. She had encountered heavy traffic on the way and was close to arriving but running a little late. I told Virginia to take her time, that we had just arrived. I asked Paul and Bob to wait for her in the driveway and point out a parking spot. I would go and meet the clients.

The twin-house owned by Sharan and Gus. The picture was taken upon our arrival on March 30, 2010. The neighbors on the right were not home during the time of our investigation.

Virginia travels from Queens, New York, to work cases with The PPA, and quite often, she arrives before the rest of the team, depending on where the investigation is located. When she does arrive first, she can usually be found busily writing down initial impressions while sitting in her car. I am always amazed by Virginia's accurate information and uncanny insight, even prior to entering a dwelling. This ritual helps Virginia "tune in" to the property and opens her up for the initial walk-through. When Virginia began working with The PPA, we provided her with an alternate location to meet so she would not know exactly where she was going. This allowed her to do a "cold reading" of the property and provided us with impressions of detected activity with no prior knowledge of the home or the family. Authenticity of the information was always protected, but after a year of meeting this way, we allowed Virginia to drive directly to the property under investigation. Because her information provided consistent accuracy case after case, she more than proved herself to our team but it was becoming redundant and time-consuming meeting elsewhere. We still advise our clients to ignore information that can be found on the internet through an address but that is typically generalized information anyway. We are looking for very intimate details of what is going on inside the house, relating to the activity and the family.

While Paul and Bob were waiting for Virginia in the driveway, I walked over to the front porch and greeted Sharan and Gus who anxiously awaited our arrival. I was happy that Virginia didn't arrive first, in this case, because once she arrives at a property that we're about to investigate, she starts receiving information -- a plethora of information! It is then very difficult for Virginia not to talk to clients about what she is receiving before

I arrive. I like to record her information on an audio recorder when she first receives it, rather than later asking
her to repeat what she has already told the clients. So in
this case, Virginia's delay gave me a chance to prepare.

Sharan and Gus invited me inside and introduced
me to the rest of their family. I explained that we
start our investigations by having Virginia do a walk-
through of the house before setting up technical gear.
This shields Virginia from the observation that a particular area may have more activity because our gear is
present. I explained that while we moved from one floor
to another, Paul and Bob would fall in behind us and
start setting up equipment in those areas. I also gave a
few warnings to Sharan and Gus, ones I give to our clients on every case. Sometimes Virginia generates a list
of many names during a walk-through. If she receives
ten names, however, that doesn't mean there are ten
ghosts in the house. It means that she is either getting
those names in the form of historical information about
someone connected to the property, or possibly there is
a spirit present trying to give Virginia their name. This
happens frequently when a spirit is somehow connected
to a person present with us. The spirit is just popping in
to say hello to someone. It could also be that someone on
the other side is talking about someone else by the name
that Virginia is receiving. She could even be getting the
name of a ghost who is at the location as well. So, with
that in mind, Virginia typically acquires many names in
various ways. Through the course of the investigation,
Virginia will then separate those names and figure out
what name belongs to the person or persons who are actually haunting the home. I have observed something of
particular interest on every investigation with Virginia.
Just like going to a medium for a reading where spirits "show up" momentarily to say hello, spirits will also

do that during our investigations. Our goal is to clear all people from a home when we investigate. The more people present, the more spirits may drop in to share information, making it more difficult for Virginia to pick up solely on those souls who may be haunting the home. This even happens for our investigators who are present, but Virginia has learned most of our deceased family and friends and can easily identify them if they show up, put them aside for the time being, and focus on the investigation.

After my brief introduction and "warnings" to Sharan and Gus and a quick tour of the house, I retrieved my audio recorder and invited Virginia inside for the initial walk-through, the process which often makes the biggest impact on our clients. The information Virginia provides in relation to the house and the clients usually makes a believer out of the biggest skeptics. We would now hear what information Virginia was receiving in real time and later be able to use that information as a starting point for the physical investigation. On a side note, much of the information presented in this book has been taken directly from the original audio recordings from this investigation, including the information gathered from the initial walk-through that you are about to read about.

During a typical walk-through, we ask Virginia to describe what type of experiences the clients are having in each room, who she thinks is there, and if she feels that there is anything we need to be concerned about during the investigation. Sometimes Virginia will receive first and last names for people and spirits; other times, just a first or last name. On occasion, Virginia will not get a name at all, but only initials, or an impression of who the ghost is, such as a male or female, or an adult or child. Virginia will usually know this by the type of energy she feels. Every case is different, and the quality of the incoming information largely depends on Virginia's physical and emotional state that day, the energy that she is working with on the other side, and the general combined energy of the location itself. I have learned that multiple factors play a role in psychic ability and the way information is processed.

When Virginia entered the house, I introduced her to Sharan and Gus in the front room where the front entry door was located. This room would be considered the living room, with a couch and chairs to the left, and a TV entertainment center to the right, positioned towards the back of a staircase which leads to the second floor. My own personal impressions when I first walked into the house was, that of a very neat and beautifully decorated home with a very warm feeling inside. A question crossed my mind. Based on all prior reports of physical activity, would this warm feeling soon go away? Only time would tell.

Virginia's First Impressions

Virginia began by revealing the impressions she had received in her car. A name kept repeatedly surfacing. The name turned out to be Sharan and Gus' son's name. Virginia said her attention was being "pulled" to the son's bedroom, the attic area, and the basement. In the short time waiting in her car, Virginia did not get any additional information on the type of activity that was happening within those areas, but she was focusing in on the right areas. Virginia sensed that someone enjoyed sitting and watching out of the attic window.

She also sensed an issue with money, or a loss of money, but couldn't be more specific on that subject.

Once Virginia covered her initial impressions with Gus and Sharan, we were ready to begin the walk-through of the interior. Sharan and Gus had arranged to take their children to a different location and would do that while we were conducting the walk-through and getting the equipment set up. The team made plans to go out for dinner and then meet Sharan and Gus back at the house before starting the active investigation. Sharan and Gus left with their family, and we began the walk-through.

Virginia's Initial Walk-Through

Dining Room & Kitchen

Once Virginia had revealed her initial impressions and Gus and Sharan had departed the house with their children, Virginia began walking through the living room, moving towards the back of the house and into the formal dining room. The dining room was just as beautifully decorated with a glass top table and the infamous chairs which were discovered many mornings placed on top of the table. Something I learned about the chairs just then, was that they were very heavy. I couldn't help but wonder if a ghost could place several heavy chairs neatly on top of a table, or if this event had a more human cause. If someone told me that their chairs were pulled out from a table, or even knocked over, that would seem more likely. Could a ghost focus enough energy to precisely move heavy chairs to the top of a table and neatly place a napkin on them? This question kept running through my mind.

Various chairs placed on top of the dining room table by an unknown source prior to the PPA investigation.

Virginia immediately began sensing a "pulling" and "very sad" energy in the dining room and kitchen. She felt the sadness was coming from someone losing a loved one in World War II. She was a wife, a very bitter woman, who did not want to move forward because of her anger towards God. Virginia told us that she could not get the name of the woman yet but was feeling a great amount of pain in her head, like she was going to have a stroke. This was not Virginia's pain, but pain associated with and being transferred from the energy of this spirit. Virginia believed that this woman's anger had eventually led her to have a stroke. Virginia explained that when she first arrived and said a few opening prayers, she heard a woman angrily say, "Don't pray! Don't pray! There is nothing to pray for. What are you praying for? There is no God!" Virginia added that she heard a few "choice words" and at the time didn't know the source. Virginia now felt it to be connected with this woman in the dining room.

Basement
Virginia wrapped up in the dining room and was being pulled towards the basement. I followed her into the basement, or more appropriately, I followed Virginia's lead as she pushed me in front of her and told me to go first. I commented, "You're the psychic!" And she responded in an elevated voice, "Yeah I know! That's why you have to go first. I'm the one who'll see something go running across the room!" Members of our team know that Virginia does not like dark basements. She enlightened me on this issue during one of our first cases together. I assumed since she worked with ghosts every day, she would be used to creepy basements after so many years. Most people get startled when it's a living person that takes them off guard, so I

understood Virginia's uneasiness. Off we went as I lead the way, Virginia right on me as we descended the stairs to the basement.

Because this was an older house, it possessed a typical old, unfinished basement atmosphere. The walls were constructed of cinder block, and the ceiling was not finished, but it had a nice, relatively clean, concrete floor. The basement was cool and very dry, which would create a more pleasant investigation later on.

When Virginia walked into the basement, she immediately picked up on the energy of a man smoking and wearing glasses. She said the man was walking around working on something. Virginia got the impression that before the house was built, the property was part of German or Dutch farmland. Virginia also picked up on the names "Felicity" and a "Bill" or "William" but did not know if they were together as a couple or separate. Virginia stated she was consciously moving forward in time and began to pick up on another male energy. She felt this person was from the 1960's and referred to him as mentally "slow." He was a male who enjoyed tinkering and playing with radios; in particular, ham radios. He seemed to be a recluse but liked to talk to people over the radio. She said he spent most of his time in the basement but didn't like all the shelves and tables that were now there. He was a bit confused as to where it all came from. Virginia felt as if these objects were intruding on his work space. He did point out to Virginia that he liked the chess game sitting on one table then confirmed that his name was William. Virginia stated that William had extreme mood swings. One moment he was fine, the next he was not. Virginia said in this moment she could feel the woman coming down the stairs, almost stomping her feet as she descended. Virginia again felt a bitter energy and believed that this angry woman had survived a stroke. As Virginia wrapped up in the basement, walking towards the stairs, she alerted me to a soldier in a grey uniform who quickly disappeared. Virginia didn't want to work on him just yet, so we left the basement.

Kitchen

As we went up the stairs and into the kitchen, Virginia described seeing many formless shadows and figures moving through the kitchen area. She described that the family may be seeing a "tremendous amount" of shadow movement. Sharan and Gus earlier confirmed that they were, in fact, seeing shadow figures moving about the first floor in the kitchen, dining room, and living room. Virginia moved from the kitchen into the dining room when she stopped abruptly, turned and looked at me, and asked, in a confused voice, "Did they practice any Voodoo?" Having no idea what she was talking about, I raised my eyebrows and said, "What do you mean?" Virginia said she was feeling that someone in the house was involved in Voodoo or had Voodoo performed on them. This was something which I had no information at all. Certainly if Voodoo were at play and Gus and Sharan knew about it, why wouldn't they tell me? Virginia was firm with her perceptions and asked me to call Sharan. "Wow!" I thought. "This is make or break the psychic time." We were just getting started, and Virginia wanted me to call and ask a question about something that rarely happens in normal situations. I was worried that Sharan would think Virginia was crazy and Gus would think she was a fake, but Virginia was sticking to it, so I was satisfied and placed a call to Sharan. With a quick "hello" from Sharan, I asked if anyone in the house had ever been involved with Voodoo or if anyone may have had Voodoo performed on them at some point. Sharan's answer... "Yeah, we think so!" Wow again! That was something I didn't expect to hear. "That's kind of important information," I explained to Sharan, then I asked if she would elaborate. Sharan said there was a private matter that they didn't want to discuss, but they believed that Santeria may have been performed on them; more specifically on Gus! Santeria is similar to Voodoo but not exactly the same. Virginia would likely want to discuss this in more detail upon their return.

Second Floor Son's Bedroom

After leaving the basement and making our way through the kitchen, Virginia felt a pull from the second floor where the family's bedrooms were located. Virginia ascended the staircase with Paul, Bob and me in tow, and she went directly to the second bedroom on the right, which is Sharan and Gus' son's bedroom. At the top of the stairs directly ahead was the second-floor bathroom. Turning around to the left and facing the opposite direction, the main second-floor hallway. The first door to the right, moving towards the front of the house, was the daughters' bedroom. This would later be our command center for the night since there was the least amount of activity happening in there. Continuing down the hallway was the son's room, and then finally the master bedroom straight ahead at the far end of the hallway.

But back to Virginia in the son's room! Sharan had reported that her son's baseball caps had been laid out neatly in a circle, a figurine in the center, and a drumstick through the neck of the figurine. Sharan had also explained that her son had frequently complained about a dark shadow figure coming in and out of his bedroom closet. From the hallway, the closet was straight ahead.

A raised bed was to the left with a little sitting area under the bed. As soon as Virginia entered the room, she felt the energy of a spirit that persistently walked in and out of the room, almost in a pacing manner. Virginia felt this spirit often leaned against the doorframe, smoking and watching. According to her vision, Virginia said this spirit enjoyed listening to music and was very curious about the music that was often playing in the room. Virginia then picked up on a type of priest or pastor energy, or someone who used to give sermons, but wasn't sure how far back she was going to pick up on this vibration. Virginia started to feel a strong church connection. She then began to experience shortness of breath as she switched back to the person who was smoking. She sensed that the smoker was a woman who liked music and had a difficult time breathing. Virginia then left the bedroom and moved down the hallway into the master bedroom.

A shot from the video camera mounted atop the son's bedroom door.

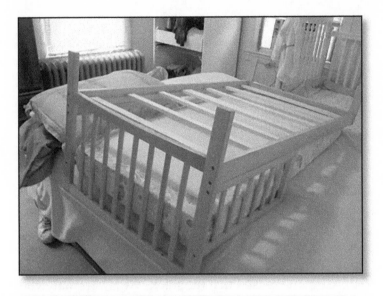

A toddler bed was discovered overturned on Sharan and Gus' bed in the master bedroom.

Master Bedroom

In the master bedroom, a door to the left concealed a staircase that lead to the attic area. On the left wall, a computer desk and a chair resided with shelves to their right. To the immediate right of the bedroom door, a queen-sized bed stood, a toddler bed hugged the right wall, and a tall dresser was placed near the foot of the bed on the front wall.

As soon as Virginia walked into the room, she looked at me and exclaimed, "Point blank! Get the f**k out of my house!" I asked Virginia who was speaking to her. Virginia replied, "Female! Very Staunch! Very angry! Get the f**k out of my house!" Virginia then took a deep breath and exhaled. Virginia explained that this woman reminded her of a TV interview she had seen years ago with actress, Betty Davis, after she had suffered a stroke. This woman was very thin and talking in slurred speech. Virginia tried to mimic the woman's speech. She told Virginia, "You need to move on. I don't have to tolerate this." Virginia said that her face was distorted as she spoke in an elevated, stern voice that kept repeating, "I don't have to tolerate this! You don't belong here! I don't know who you are. I'm bad enough already, and I have to deal with those children!" Virginia described the sound as "guttural" and that hearing this woman speak gave her a chill. Virginia was then pulled to the attic area, so we followed her.

Third Floor/Attic

I never know what to expect when walking into an attic. Some are dark, dirty, unfinished, and often cold and uninsulated. Others are cluttered and packed to the ceilings with years of junk. Gus and Sharan's attic had been finished and converted into two small warm, comfortable rooms: one for musical instruments on the backside of the house; the other, a small library with a sitting area. A very narrow hallway separated the two. Both had a single window with plenty of light during the day, much nicer than the typical attic.

Once Virginia entered the attic, she began receiving impressions of a spirit who enjoyed sermons and singing, chorus and organ playing. Virginia wondered if this was the angry woman she earlier located in the dining room. Virginia felt that this woman had stopped going to church. She closed her eyes for a moment then exclaimed, "Yes! Yes! She's the one!" Virginia explained that she was getting the name "Felicity" or "Frances" but couldn't get her proper name. Virginia told us that this woman used to play the organ and sing at her church, but when her husband died in World War II, everything died for her. Virginia felt that she was VERY angry at

God, had quit going to church and stopped playing music, although she still loved to listen to music. Virginia was then able to confirm this was the same spirit she felt in the son's bedroom, the one leaning against the door smoking and having a hard time breathing. This concluded Virginia's initial walk-through, so we headed back downstairs to the dining room, eager to complete the setup of our technical equipment and to get some dinner.

Chapter 4

The Investigation Begins

Because of the size of the house and the amount of activity, this walk-through took more time than usual. By the time we finished, we had a clear idea of where to set up our equipment. Virginia's information closely matched what Gus and Sharan had told us, and there were several main areas of the house where we wanted to focus — the basement, the kitchen, the son's room and the attic. Because Sharan told us that the entire family would often leave the house and later return to find rooms in disarray, I wanted to set up our infrared video cameras and audio recorders and let them run for an hour with no one in the home. My goal was to see if anything would happen while we were gone and how the house would react once we returned. For those not familiar with infrared video cameras, they are often used for commercial and home security cameras because they have the ability to "see" in the dark. An area being illuminated by infrared light remains dark to the human eye, but the features of the camera allow a room to be visible to the camera, as if the lights were on. In reality, the lights are on, but just infrared light, and infrared is a light spectrum that the human eye cannot see, so the room still appears dark to the human eye.

We began to setup our equipment just like every other case — video cameras and DVR recording system first. Only this time, we needed to be sure our video cameras were covering the front and rear doors of the house to make sure no one came in. I began setting up the DVR recorder and monitor in the daughters' bedroom on the second-floor, our makeshift command center, and Paul and Bob began to set up the cameras. Paul placed the first camera in the rear room of the attic and pointed it across the hallway to see into the front room. That nearly covered the entire attic. In the master bedroom, the next camera was set up in the back-right corner facing the bedroom door, making it possible to see much of the bedroom, some of the hallway, and the door and first couple of steps leading to the attic. Next, a camera was placed on a camera mount designed to sit atop a bedroom door, and here, it was placed on the door to the son's bedroom facing the back of the room. This would allow us to monitor the closet where the shadow figure was reported to come and go. The last camera set-up came with an interesting and startling experience. While Bob was placing the camera on a camera pole in the dining room, he let out an audible expletive. We all heard it, so obviously we wanted to know what happened. Bob reported that as he was setting up the pole, he felt someone give him a shove, almost knocking him over. Other than the psychic activity that Virginia was receiving, this was the first physical sign that something might be going on in the house. Noted! Bob finished setting up the camera, and we were live with all hardwired cameras. One additional camera was placed in a position to observe the front door while we were at dinner but then we utilized it in other areas after our return.

Once the cameras were recording, our next step was to place additional stationary equipment in areas where we might capture a physical event. Equipment such as motion alarms, laser lines, and motion activated IR cameras were also positioned in different areas throughout the home.

After all equipment was up and running, we gathered in the living room for a quick briefing on what Virginia had discovered through her psychic work. We secured the house, locked the doors, and activated the voice recorders placed throughout the house. At 8:00 p.m., everyone left the residence with no one remaining inside. It was time to get some dinner!

Since a small child, watching people has always been a trait of mine. I watch their mannerisms. I listen to what they are saying and how they are saying it. I try to see things from their perspective. I have thus learned much about interconnected relationships present in a home with an involved haunting. How the living affect the dead. How the dead affect the living. And sometimes, how people can take advantage of other people using a haunting as a means to an end.

While at dinner, another case that The PPA had investigated surfaced and reminded me of this case. Like Upper Darby, physical activity had also been reported when everyone was out of the house. In that investigation, we also removed everyone from the house for an hour and let the equipment run. One of the family's biggest complaints involved furniture being moved all the time and items such as jewelry, watches, medication, and money going missing, never to be seen again. During dinner, something interesting happened. Over the hour we spent with the family, I watched the behavior of the clients' teenage daughter change. She became quiet and restless, endlessly scratching herself and fidgeting. As a Pennsylvania State Trooper, I had worked with hundreds of drug abusers throughout the years and recognized the signs of withdrawal. I started to suspect that what we had on our hands was a drug addict stealing from her parents and faking a haunting. Sure enough, we were able to capture the daughter, on video and audio, manipulating items in the home and reporting them as ghostly activity. At the conclusion of that investigation, we advised the parents of our findings, and they approached their daughter. The daughter subsequently confessed to having a drug addiction and stealing the items.

That situation was similar to the Upper Darby case, only in that the family was reporting activity happening while they were not home. Through dinner, however, I did think about the possibility of someone manipulating items in the house, and I wanted to watch for that as we continued forward with the investigation. Something that became very clear, when later sitting down and speaking with Gus and Sharan, was that they were two intelligent people who were only concerned about their family and were completely sincere about what they were telling us. They had endured activity for nearly three years, often without the children even being present, escalating to the point where they could no longer bear it and were willing to try anything to get rid of it. Both came from different religious backgrounds and had their own unique opinions about the occurrences, but both agreed that they needed to find answers for the safety of their children. Gus told me after dinner that even though he was experiencing this ordeal, he still had a hard time believing it was happening. He was not a strong believer in ghosts but didn't know what else to think. Like many other people we have worked with, the house seemed to be changing his mind. We kept the conversation about the haunting to a minimum because Virginia was present with us at that time, and again, we did not want to contaminate her with information.

Now back to the investigation! When returning to the house, I incorrectly was filled with anticipation to discover any activity while we were gone. As I've stated earlier, it's one of our teachings to NOT anticipate anything on an investigation, but I was certainly eager to see if anything happened. It was now 8:59 p.m., and an hour had passed. Gus and Sharan had not yet returned. I unlocked the door, and Virginia and I went inside. Unfortunately, it looked like a whole lot of nothing went on while we were out. Taking a quick walk through the living room into the dining room, nothing was out of place. But just as Paul and Bob came walking in the front door, we heard a very loud bang coming from upstairs. Not the type of bang that occurs on a cold night when the air temperature causes wood to pop, but more like something large had fallen and hit the floor with a thud. I thought someone was in the house, for sure, so Bob and Paul ran upstairs to see if they could find anything. Nothing seemed to be out of place, and nobody was in the house. Maybe we were just receiving a warm welcome home!

After Sharan and Gus returned and all were settled in, we escorted them to our command area where they would sit during the investigation. All lights were turned off in the house and the team separated into two — Mark and Virginia would be one team, and Paul and Bob would be the other. It was now 9:15 p.m., and we were more than ready to begin the physical investigation.

With Virginia's prior information in my thoughts, I started working on a strategy for investigating. A woman named Felicity, or other prominent "F" name, existed; she was angry, liked music, didn't like kids, and likely had endured a stroke. A male named William lived in the home; he was not "right in the head," as Virginia put it, but he liked tinkering with electronics. A soldier was briefly spotted in the basement during the walk-through, but Virginia wasn't feeling him in the house anymore. I had a variety of ways to interact with each of the spirits Virginia had identified. My first objective was to elicit a physical response or see if they would talk with Virginia so we could understand why they were still there. One of the main goals of our physical investigation, along with documenting physical activity, was to identify the culprits haunting the house, determine why they stayed there, or find out their origin if not immediately connected to the property somehow. If we could gather this information, we could then later work with it to help remove the spirits from the property, or help them in a variety of other ways.

The PPA investigates in different ways depending on the size of the location and the amount of equipment needed. A rather large structure, even though it was a twin-home, we knew that our team required four people. Gus and Sharon decided to stay in the home throughout the investigation, so we utilized them as well. They were confined to our command center behind a closed door where we could account for them, so we put them to work monitoring our video monitor. We normally have one team monitor the video cameras while the second is out investigating, but in this situation, we utilized Gus and Sharon to watch the cameras and report any unusual activity while both teams were investigating different floors of the home.

For our first rotation, Paul and Bob were assigned to investigate the second floor while Virginia and I would cover the basement. When we investigate buildings that have at least three floors and a basement, we sometimes

have two teams actively investigating if we can be separated by a floor acting as a sound barrier. That was the
case in this house, so the four of us made a quick visit together, to the two attic rooms, before we ventured to our
assigned areas. Virginia immediately encountered the
angry woman in the front room and gathered additional information about her. Virginia was now certain that
this woman was left to raise a mentally handicapped
boy (William) by herself after her husband was killed
in World War II. Virginia sensed that the husband had
been a pilot whose plane was shot down during the war.
Virginia believed William had severe mood swings,
and his mother had a difficult time dealing with him.
William was also the male in the basement, according
to Virginia, who liked to tinker with electronics; he was
now in his adult years. With this new information, we
left Paul and Bob would work with the woman, and
Virginia and I headed down to the basement to find
William.

Once back in the basement, Virginia immediately
started receiving impressions of William being present
with us, and he seemed to be curious about my video
camera. Virginia saw him checking out the EMF meter I
had just placed on a table. An EMF meter is a device that
identifies and measures the strength of an electromag-
netic field. Any device or wire with electricity flowing
through it emits an EMF field. When we enter a room,
we can perform a sweep to see where these manmade
fields are present. Paranormal investigators then watch
for spontaneous EMF spikes, which often occur in con-
junction with paranormal events. Virginia confirmed
that this spirit was named "William," so I attempted
to get William to interact with me by having him try
to manipulate my EMF meter, along with a variety of
other objects in the basement. All requests to make

something physical happen failed. With no sign of the soldier that Virginia had previously seen, after nearly thirty minutes in the basement I contacted Paul and Bob via walkie-talkie and advised them to meet us back at command.

Once returning to command, we conducted a post-rotation debriefing, as we do on every investigation. Virginia reported on her findings in the basement, but I had nothing of significance to report from a technical point of view. Paul, however, had a few interesting experiences from the second floor. While in the master bedroom, Paul was video recording an EMF meter he had laid on the bed. Trying to get someone to interact with it and watching for a change in the EMF reading, something grabbed Paul's wrist and turned the video camera. Paul said, in that moment, he audibly offered for anyone who may be interested to check out his camera, or touch it, and then it felt like someone physically moved his wrist. The time was 10:02 p.m. Shortly after experiencing the movement of his wrist, Paul reported that the area directly around him became very cold, even though he was sitting on a heated radiator. Bob confirmed that the air temperature had dropped around Paul, and the room was colder. Roughly ten minutes later, Bob put a small flashlight on the floor and turned it on. This type of flashlight has a push button bottom to "click" the light on and off. After laying it on the floor, Bob requested for anyone that might be there with them to roll the flashlight across the floor. A few moments later, as Paul was still filming, the flashlight began to dim, almost to the point where no light was visible. Paul told Bob to check his flashlight, and instantly, the light turned back on to full brightness. As Paul was finished explaining these events, Virginia immediately said, "It's William!" and then explained that she felt it was William looking at the equipment that caused the light to dim.

Remember that earlier in the night, Virginia had told us that William loved to tinker with electronics and was curious about my equipment in the basement. Virginia sensed that William was looking at Paul's camera when Paul had invited anyone to touch it, and then he played with Bob's flashlight a short time later. This revelation made sense, but I wanted to document more definitive information from a technical perspective. The final piece of information during our debriefing was from Gus. He reported that he observed seeing the door to his son's bedroom slightly close at 9:50 p.m. while watching our video monitor. Since we had hard wired the cameras and taped down the cables, I assumed that someone had stepped on the cable or that the door was not well-balanced and had moved because of gravity. Whatever it was, I opened the door all the way and wedged it against the wall with our cord reel. A few tugs on the cable proved that the door would not be moved if someone stepped on or tugged the cable. With that issue resolved, it was time for the second rotation.

During the second rotation, I sent Virginia with Bob to the first floor, and Paul and I went to the third-floor attic rooms. Although Paul and I spent a considerable amount of time trying coax someone on the other side to communicate with us, it remained quiet in the attic. Paul and I spent some time trying to debunk the keyboard that Sharan had previously reported playing by itself, but we could not get it to make any noise on its own. We then very poorly tried playing music since we knew the angry woman liked music. Neither Paul nor I were musically inclined, so we probably stirred her anger even further with the cacophony! Neither of the attic rooms revealed any activity, so when our time for that rotation ended, we headed back down to command, hoping that some type of activity would appear on one of our audio recorders during the review.

When we reached command, I was once again surprised that the other team had experienced some activity during their investigation. A lack of personal experiences seemed to be a developing pattern for me on this investigation, but I was happy to discover that my team members were, at least, experiencing a few things Gus and Sharan had reported. More importantly, additional information was being gathered. Bob disclosed that while he and Virginia were sitting in the dining room, the video camera he placed on the dining room table had shut off on its own. Bob turned it back on to start recording again, and within a few, it turned off again. Our team has never experienced a problem with this camera, and it had never turned itself off while recording unless the battery died, or the user had failed to hit the record button. Bob checked, and it was recording at the time it turned off. The battery was near full-charge and not an issue, so we were perplexed but we have previously experienced various, weird electrical malfunctions with other electronic devices and recorders on other cases. It was another small, peculiar occurrence to add to several others! Virginia's report was a little more profound. As she was sitting with Bob in the dining room, she was psychically picking-up on someone talking to her about money being stolen. She and Bob then heard what sounded like a quarter being thrown against a wall in the living room. The time now was 11:04 p.m. Virginia and Bob moved into the living room a few minutes, looking for a quarter or something similar. While looking around the room, Virginia audibly commented, "I see no games going on! There's nothing happening here! No games! Nothing being turned on!" At that moment, both Bob and Virginia heard what sounded like a toy or game making a musical sound. I'm not sure what intrigued me more — the fact that they heard what they thought was a quarter being thrown against something, as reported by Sharan and Gus to happen frequently, or the fact that a toy made a musical sound, right when Virginia stated the opposite. But that was not the worst of it. After spending time in the living room investigating the different sounds, Virginia and Bob sat back down at the dining room table. Virginia told us that she closed her eyes and took a deep breath to help her tune in to the events, and at that moment, she felt like someone was choking her. Paul and I could hear Virginia from upstairs at that time and commented that some activity must be happening. Virginia seemed to be yelling at someone, which occasionally happened on these cases, but unless Virginia specifically calls for us, we usually just let her keep going. We were certainly curious to hear what she had to report, however, I wasn't quite expecting to hear that she had been attacked. Virginia acknowledged that when she closed her eyes and began to "tune in" it felt like someone had put a bag over her head and pulled it backwards. Furthermore, she was being choked and had to break the connection from the energy. Subsequently, the choking feeling went away. Virginia became angry and yelled, "Never do that again!" She wasn't sure which spirit was involved, but Virginia felt a masculine energy that was somehow related to the Voodoo. While we were still on break, I walked past the son's bedroom to adjust a piece of equipment in the master bedroom. As I was passing the doorway, I noticed that the cord reel used to wedge open the son's door had been moved. I checked the tape holding down the video cable in the hallway, and the cord had not been pulled, so I wasn't sure why the door would have moved. Although I trusted that neither Sharan nor Gus would tamper with our equipment, I made a mental note to check the recorders and verify that neither of them had left the room for any reason. What I later discovered was, they had not.

Sometimes when we investigate, I will move teammates around so investigators can work with Virginia at different periods in the night. This was the case at the Upper Darby home. From previous experience, we have found that some ghosts will react differently to different investigators. Since Virginia was picking up on at least three separate ghosts in this house, I wanted each of the investigators to have a turn working with her to see if she would report any differences, or different reactions, to a particular investigator. When that occurs, we have discovered that the individual will likely be our best resource for obtaining additional information from a ghost then later helping them "crossover." On the next investigative rotation, I wanted Paul to work with Virginia on the second floor while Bob and I went to the basement to see if "William" would play with some of our equipment, since Virginia reported he liked to "tinker" with equipment.

Once in the basement, Bob and I scattered a variety of equipment around the room to elicit any type of reaction. We placed Bob's flashlight on the concrete floor. Multiple EMF meters were stationed on tables and shelves in several different areas of the basement, and a motion activated light was placed at the opposite end of the room than where we were working. The light was positioned in a way that we wouldn't set it off ourselves, but it would still pick up any movement on the stairs and that part of the basement. After thirty minutes, I heard Bob's video camera click-off. Bob let out the old, "What the Hell?" and I knew something was amiss. Bob told me his recorder had turned itself off again. This was the third time the recorder had turned off during this investigation. Bob turned the camera back on and rewound it a few seconds to make sure it was recording prior to shutting off. It had been recording up until the point it seemingly had shut itself off. Some recorders, including this one, have timers that will shut down to save battery life. We double checked, just to make sure that wasn't the case, but it seemed that everything was working and recording properly up to that point. Just one more strange occurrence to add to the list.

Virginia and Paul finished their rotation on the second floor after spending additional time in the son's bedroom and the master bedroom. No noticeable physical events occurred during their time in each room, but Virginia was able to gather more information on who she felt was in the house and why they were agitated. We all met back at command to take a short break. While I stepped out, Virginia held a short discussion with Gus and Sharan about the Voodoo incident performed on Gus. During their conversation, Virginia learned about personal issues between Gus and a few acquaintances. She then determined that a spell to financially and physically break Gus may have been cast on him by one of these people who practiced Santeria. Sharan told Virginia that they were, in fact, having financial issues with their business. Virginia told Gus and Sharan that she felt something stronger occurring than just a spell cast for financial issues, that this went beyond Santeria, and that someone had conjured up a negative entity and "sent" it to Gus. Virginia also sensed that a heart binding ceremony was performed on Gus. The chilling part? Sharan told Virginia that Gus had been in the hospital with four minor heart attacks since they had learned a spell may have been cast on him. Gus and Sharan verified that this dark entity seemed to revolve around Gus, and we now believed that, along with a possible haunting, a negative attachment was present.

Once Virginia was done speaking with Gus and Sharan, she met with me outside to talk over a potential game plan for resolving the haunting. Resolving a haunting depends on many factors, such as whether the clients are with us at the time, if we have any negative energies that concern us, the personality of any ghost that may be present and their state of mind, how many spirits are present, and how safe we feel tackling any particular resolution with our assigned team. Each experience is different, and diverse spirits interact with investigators in many ways, just like the living. In this particular case, many factors existed, which included consideration for all of the above and more. Additionally, we needed to sit down and discuss these factors with Sharan and Gus. It was 11:40 p.m. when Virginia and I came back inside. We sat down with Sharan and Gus, giving them our assessment. Our team had experienced a variety of activity. Bob's video camera strangely turned off three times while actively investigating. His flashlight went nearly completely out and then popped back on when Paul told Bob to look at it while they were investigating the master bedroom. Paul's wrist and camera moved when something grabbed it, twisting it back and forth. Paul also reported that while sitting on a heated radiator, the room became very cold. Bob confirmed that the air around Paul was cold. While Virginia and Bob were on the first floor, they both heard what sounded like a quarter being thrown against something in the living room. When they went in the living room to investigate, they heard a few musical tones, as if a toy had switched on, just as Virginia spoke about not seeing any games or toys turning on. And most disturbing, Virginia felt that a negative force had pulled her head back and choked her while she was sitting at the dining room table.

After discussing our game plan, Virginia and I felt that our best approach was to have the team sit down at the dining room table and work on crossing over the two spirits — that of the angry woman and that of her mentally handicapped adult son. Once we felt they were safely out of the house, we could start working on the negative entity attached to Gus. I asked Virginia if the angry woman was aware of and communicating with her son. Virginia sensed that they were on two different levels, or frequencies, and that the son had no idea that his mother was still in the house in some form. Virginia also perceived that when the mother died, she stayed to help her son because of his mental impairment. After the son had passed, he stayed because it was his home. But neither of them was able to connect with the other, according to Virginia, and they were locked in this dreamlike state, going on with their daily lives and not questioning their existence. Virginia explained that the mother recognized her son was in the house, but she was not able to communicate with him. Virginia had initial concerns that on this visit she may not be able to completely remove the dark entity attached to Gus because she was not always feeling it present.

Another potential issue with which we are sometimes faced is the interconnected energy and attachment between the spirit and the living person. Many factors on behalf of the living can make it difficult to remove an attachment, but we could not discern the effectiveness until after our work was complete. We explained to Gus and Sharan that we were going to work on the attachment also, but if we needed to come back, specifically to deal with that issue, we would do so. Our team keeps in weekly contact with our clients over the two weeks following an investigation in case something should happen after we leave, but for this night, we would see how effective we could be at clearing everything from the house.

Paul, Bob, Virginia, and I sat down around the dining room table; the lights dimmed. Virginia lit a white candle which she placed in the middle of the table and then said a few prayers for protection, guidance, and assistance. When we perform a cleansing, Virginia asks those investigators assisting her to close their eyes and visualize pulling in white light as we take slow, deep breaths to increase the amount of positive energy in the room. Virginia stated that the angry woman was with us, so she would first work with her. After a few moments, Virginia relayed that the woman was giving her a hard time and did not want to go, so we switched gears and decided to work on releasing her son. Once Virginia connected with the son, she was able to pull him near her and communicate to him that he had passed on. Virginia told him that she was going to try and connect him with his mother. Immediately, Virginia saw the mother waiting for her son, and the woman said that if Virginia could convince him to move into the light, she would be there to move on with him. Otherwise, the woman was not leaving without her son. It took time, but eventually, Virginia was able to earn his trust, and he moved forward into the light, as Virginia described it to us, and mother and son were gone.

I always ask Virginia what she sees when someone "moves into the light." Virginia has explained a multitude of ways that ghosts leave this world and move on to the next level. Once Virginia makes a connection with a spirit, she asks for divine guidance from the other side. Sometimes she will see a spec of light or a whole column of light appear. Sometimes the "doorway" will look like an illuminated bridge and other times like a gentle vortex of light. Virginia has related on occasion that she will just ask her spirit guides, angels, or family members of a ghost to come for that soul, and she always sees someone appear who is willing to help. I often think it must be amazing to experience something like this, but I have not been blessed with that ability. Not yet anyway!

With the two human spirits out of the house, the time came to tackle the negative entity that had choked Virginia and seemed to be attached to Gus. Sometimes we witness a simple, quick detachment, and other times the detachment proves difficult. Much of the success depends on the willingness of the victim to do what is necessary to sever the detachment. Virginia did not sense this entity in the house anymore, so this could be a problem. This seemed to be the norm throughout the entire investigation. Virginia had picked up on the angry woman being the strongest energy present, then the son, but the negative entity seemed to be present one moment and gone the next. In fact, Virginia stated that the angry woman's energy was so strong that it may have held the negative entity at bay. Virginia felt that the woman was not only angry, bitter, and controlling, but she also had an extremely dominant personality. Virginia also sensed that this woman was the spirit knocking things over and pulling items off shelves. Whenever this spirit would become angry at Gus' and Sharan's family, she would react physically, especially after an argument or much noise and commotion by the children. This sort of event occurred many times after the family had all left because they were no longer there to scream at. Not that the family could hear her anyway.

Since Virginia could not pick up on the negative entity nor pull it toward her, we decided to take the approach of prayer and energy work, along with any divine guidance we could get. Virginia started with a few extra prayers of protection for our team, Gus and Sharan, with a little extra prayer work specifically for Gus. Virginia asked for some guidance from her "team" on the other side and called on her guides and angels to help remove and return the entity to its source. Virginia was not feeling the negative entity present at the time, so she could not be certain if we were successful in removing the attachment. We would have to see what happened in the next few days, but we were hopeful.

After concluding at the dining room table, Virginia and I started doing additional energy work around the house. This included a few techniques such as saging, spraying holy water, and employing several house cleansing visualization techniques integrating Reiki energy for healing the home, an esoteric form of using subtle energies to change the vibration in a particular space. Thought is energy, and on a quantum level, thought can influence the environment. The intended outcome was to remove any negative vibrational energy and replace it with positive energy, which would hopefully help the family heal in numerous ways, including getting their peaceful home back.

While Virginia and I finished the cleansing, Paul and Bob packed up the investigative equipment and packed the van. The last thing to do was speak with Gus and Sharan one more time. We gathered in the living room to discuss the night's investigation. Several things that our team experienced matched what the family had reported, but we also captured many hours of audio and video recordings. We thoroughly review every recording made on every investigation, and this process can often add up to more review time than the hours put in at a full-time job. The PPA's policies dictate that we review all our recordings within ten days with an additional four days for follow-up review and analysis on anything that we discern to have a paranormal cause. In any event, we make every attempt to complete our review in two weeks and get back to our clients with our findings at the end of those two weeks. In between, I always check-in with clients three days after our visit to make sure everything is okay and to get feedback on the current level of activity, if any. Three days has always been a good gauge for something additional to happen, if anything is going to happen. If all is quiet, we are hopeful that things will continue that way, and we continue with our review. If activity persists, we re-evaluate and occasionally need to do some additional work. Virginia did one more walk-through of the house with Sharan, and everyone present agreed the home felt much "lighter" than before. The recorders assigned to investigators for review were provided to Paul, Bob, and me, and our vehicles were packed and ready to go. We said our goodbyes and departed to start the two-and-a-half-hour ride home. It was now 1:00 a.m.

The conversation was much different on the ride home as Paul, Bob, and I discussed their physical experiences, the insights that Virginia provided, and what we would find during the review. Reflecting on the night, although there were some weird physical events that occurred, I was disappointed that we were not able to document items pulled off shelves or thrown around the house for the hour that we were out for dinner. It would have been great to obtain video footage of what was causing the mess. We certainly were not disappointed with what did happen throughout the night, however, and we were now looking forward to starting the review of the Upper Darby investigation. I couldn't wait to review the recordings!

Chapter 5

Review & Analysis

The toughest part of any investigation, in my opinion, has always been the review where we scrutinize and listen to copious hours of recorded audio and video, along with analyzing still photographs collected during the investigation. Although there is a momentary rush of excitement when something stands out beyond the normal, pouring over so many hours of recordings becomes quite tedious. Given that the team was out late the night before, we used Saturday as a "down day" to recuperate. A good review can't effectively be executed when one is tired, so we try to get adequate sleep before jumping in. For me, the day after an investigation historically has been the day when I unload equipment from the vehicle and get it repackaged properly and ready for the next case. On days when I've tried to jump into a review when tired, my mind has wandered, and I have even fallen asleep while listening to a recording. Some of the sounds we are looking for are so faint or so fast that if our attention strays from the recording for just a few seconds, we might miss something. Alertness is vital!

The PPA has a process in place for reviewing recordings. When we activate the stationary recorders at the onset of an investigation, all are started at the same time to synchronize the chronological counter of each recorder. We also try to synchronize the actual time as closely as possible. The recorders are set in place for each investigation, inside and out, and we now have many devices to later compare sounds and voices against should we capture something on one device.

We begin our review individually as each investigator assigned to a case listens to the recorder, or recorders, that are assigned to him or her. If an investigator identifies something that may contain potential evidence of the paranormal, that investigator must then compare it with any additional recording equipment to which he has been assigned. His task involves ruling out the sound or video anomaly first. If not possible, it gets marked for later analysis. If the investigator identifies the anomaly as having a manmade cause, it is discarded. Any anomaly marked for later analysis will be reviewed by other members who were involved in the investigation. It will then be the other investigators' job to compare the anomaly with all recorders to which they were assigned and identify or rule out the anomaly themselves. If the anomaly still cannot be ruled out, it is discussed by the investigation team and likely presented to the clients as documented evidence when no other cause can be found.

Once Sunday arrived, Paul, Bob, and I started listening to the recorders when something that has never occurred during a PPA review happened. I started receiving messages from Paul and Bob indicating that they were getting all kinds of sounds on their recorders. This was something I was experiencing myself. To my disbelief, during the hour that we had left the house for dinner, all of our recording equipment had picked up activity. The house sounded like a circus. So much commotion erupted, it was hard to believe that people weren't making the noise. As I reviewed my audio recorder, I was also watching the DVR recording from the stationary cameras we had placed around the house. Both recordings are synced so I can see what is going on while I am listening to the audio recorder. I could easily see that no one was in the home, but we had more than fifty anomalous noises recorded. Minor sounds like creeks and cracks were heard as well as more extreme sounds like stomping footsteps up and down the first to second floor staircase and hard banging on what sounded like wood. The sounds were so numerous, logging them all became quite a task. Many of the sounds appeared to be redundant. A squeaking followed by a metal clank occurred over and over. A sound, like footsteps, was heard in many parts of the home. The hardwood floors seemed to squeak in various areas as well. The one thing I found most amazing, was the recurring sound of a quarter hitting something, as if being thrown against a hard object. We didn't notice anything physically out of place when we returned from dinner Friday night, but man, I thought, something was definitely going on inside that house when no one was home. I've never heard anything like it, and up to the writing of this book, I still have not heard so much continuous noise within one hour during an investigation. It was remarkable! In fact, we ended up with so many redundant sounds that I stopped logging and consolidated them into one or two examples of each type of sound that we could eventually use on our website. We later gave Gus and Sharan the whole recording of that hour, rather than trying to copy each individual sound. I attempted to find some type of movement in the video and was getting frustrated that I could not see anything moving anywhere. It was extraordinary to have all these sounds by themselves, but if I could find something moving, seemingly on its own, that would be even better. For the most part, I could not detect movement until I reviewed the audio recorder from the master bedroom. At 8:16 p.m., I heard very loudly what sounded like a coin hit something solid. I played that portion of the video back a few times, and finally, I observed a fast-moving quarter flying across the room near the foot of the bed, just above the floor, and hit the bottom leg assembly of a computer chair in the bedroom. The coin hit the chair then dropped to the floor. We were finally able to verify that quarters were, in fact, being thrown throughout the house, just as Gus and Sharan had reported. This physical activity also verified their claims that items were found scattered on the floor when they returned home. Sounds are very different than physical movement, so this incident finally documented that physical movement was occurring.

An image from our video camera in the master bedroom during our first investigation. The quarter that impacted the computer chair can be seen in the picture sitting on the floor, directly under the legs.

After our return to the house that Friday night, our recorders certainly picked up additional sounds while we were present. The sound of quarters being thrown into objects was one of the most prominent sounds. We couldn't figure out the origin of where they were coming from or who was throwing them, but during the investigation we did note that quarters were lying around the house in various places. The audio recorder also validated Virginia's and Bob's experience in the living room. At the time they heard a quarter hitting something, they were unable to find a quarter anywhere, but on the recording, you can plainly hear a coin hitting something and Virginia and Bob reacting to it. The same recorder also captured the musical tones that went off when Virginia was explaining to Bob that "nothing" was turning on. So far, this was turning out to be a very active location, and we were lucky to have recorded so much in one evening.

Audio evidence was not the only thing we seemed to have captured on Friday night. As I worked my way through the video from our stationary cameras, I looked forward to reviewing the time period where Gus had pointed out his son's bedroom door closing when he was watching the video monitor. I was hoping to see some type of event that caused the door to move and frankly expected it to be caused by one of us if only by accident. What I didn't expect to find, even before I got to the portion of the video with the door movement, totally blew my mind. At 9:50 p.m., the shadow of a person's upper torso entered the room from the hallway and took off to the left in a flash, then disappeared. As I was following our time-log of the investigation, I knew no one was in that area at the time. I watched the video clip over and over but could not come up with a logical answer for the cause. I even went so far as to double check all the audio recorders placed in or surrounding that room, and no one was present. When investigators previously walked into that room or even walked down the hallway past the room, distinct movement and footsteps could be heard. When the shadow figure appeared, there was no sound present at all. This event would play a much more significant role later on in this investigation, but for now, it was another piece of evidence that backed up the family's claims. In this case, the son was complaining about seeing a dark figure coming in and out of his room, sometimes moving from the closet to the hallway or vice versa. We may have caught what he was seeing!

When I reached the area of the recording to check activity with the bedroom door, I observed the door closing. Nothing that I could see would have caused the door to move. What Gus didn't see when watching the video monitor, was that a few minutes after the door had closed, it also appeared to have reopened all the way on its own. A short time later on the video, it is obvious that we were in the room working on the door and wedging the cord reel up against it. We had secured the door in a way that if someone should step or tug on the camera's video cable, it wouldn't affect the camera or the door. To my surprise, later in the investigation, the door partially closed with much more intensity and immediately reopened. During the investigation we knew something had moved the cord reel again. This is when I walked by and noticed the cord reel had been moved in the son's room, but nobody had observed the door move. The door likely reopened at that time from the recoil of the cable pulling on it. What closed it was the question! We now knew how the cord reel had been moved, but what moved the door? Furthermore, I discovered when going through the video, that the door closed and opened several more times over the course of the evening. We had verified and accounted for everyone, knowing that no one was present in that area when the door moved. It was another confirmation of the clients' accurate reporting.

When Paul reviewed his video camera footage, he observed events that occurred in the master bedroom when he and Bob were investigating the second floor. On the recording, you can plainly see that Paul's camera moves in sharp, jerky movements as if someone is turning the camera to look at each side of it. Paul reported that it felt like someone had grabbed his wrist and turned it back and forth. His stunned reaction to the event can be heard on the recording. Immediately after the event, Paul stated that he felt cold although he was sitting on a radiator, which was giving off heat. Bob confirmed that the air around Paul was definitely colder than the other areas of the room. Paul measured a significant and consistent drop in temperature with the use of an ambient air thermometer. But after considering all the factors, Paul realized he had pulled the thermometer out of his warm pants pocket and had no idea of the room's baseline temperature. These kinds of things must be factored into investigations in order to achieve valid evidence. The thermometer may have been dropping to room temperature and adjusting because of Paul's warm pocket, or it could have been dropping because of the cold spot surrounding Paul, or likely both. At any rate, we had to exclude that measurement, but it was a good lesson and future reminder for our team to keep thermometers out of warm pockets.

We carefully reviewed the rest of our recordings and were satisfied that nothing remained to work on. The team discussed and took into consideration all of our personal experiences during the investigation, the evidence documented, and Virginia's insights, and then unanimously concluded that a haunting had taken place at the home, although Virginia had no doubt from her perspective, after our visit. Over the course of the two weeks that it took to conduct the review and analysis of the investigation, I also kept in contact with Sharan. Three days after our visit, I called Sharan, spoke with her and received a good report. Everything seemed to have quieted down, and no activity was observed in the house. Sharan stated that everyone had been sleeping peacefully and things were calm. Near the end of the two weeks, I called Sharan again to advise her that we were finishing up our review and wanted to set up a date to return and review our findings. We scheduled our return visit for the following weekend. Sharan advised me that all was still quiet in the house — exactly what I wanted to hear!

The following weekend, Virginia accompanied me to the Upper Darby house, something that she doesn't normally do, but in this case, we had another investigation scheduled not far from Sharan's and Gus' home later that night, and Virginia wanted to do an in-person "check" on the house to make sure that she didn't miss anything. If there was anything else she felt necessary to do, we could also cover that while there. We had acquired much evidence and wanted to thoroughly cover everything with Gus and Sharan. Since they were already in a fragile state, we needed to take a careful, matter-of-fact approach in presenting the evidence. I have watched clients break down and fall apart when providing them with much less evidence than we were about to show Gus and Sharan, and we didn't know exactly how they would react.

Once we arrived at the Upper Darby house and were invited inside, I first noticed many smiling faces. That vision stuck with me, and I thought it to be a very good sign that things were moving in the right direction. We sat down with Sharan and Gus at the dining room table, and I set up my laptop to present audio and video evidence. I was extremely pleased to see that there were no breakdowns, but rather, they showed a disposition of affirmation. In other words, their experiences were now confirmed by people outside their inner circle; they seemed to be relieved that they weren't going crazy, that someone else not only believed them but had encountered similar experiences, and that things may be ok. It was an affirmation that attested to their real experiences. Being intelligent, business-oriented people, they appeared to appreciate the evidence for what it was, and many personal beliefs were confirmed. After we wrapped-up the review with Sharan and Gus, Virginia and I took a walk around the house. Virginia wanted to psychically "feel" around to see if she could pick up on anything that may be present that shouldn't be. All felt good to Virginia, so I was hopeful that our job here was finished and the family could finally get on with their lives. Little did I know on that visit that this would not be the case, and we would once again be returning to Upper Darby.

Chapter 6

The Hat Man

Several weeks had passed since the investigation at Sharan and Gus' home, and everything seemed to be going fine. But on one particular day, I received the email from Sharan that I hoped would never come. I always had a lingering feeling that we weren't finished with this case that easily, and here we were. Sharan wrote that on the evening of April 24, 2010, the family had retired upstairs after a late dinner. Gus heard their cat hissing and growling downstairs in the kitchen followed by what sounded like a pan hitting the floor. Sharan and her son went to investigate and discovered the lid to a pot in the middle of the kitchen floor. Almost all of the kitchen cabinets and drawers had been opened.

Pictures from the night Sharan and her son investigated the sound of a pot falling in the kitchen while the family was upstairs getting ready for bed.

From experience gained by investigating so many cases, I knew that the activity was probably not from the angry woman or her son. Virginia was confident that she had released them from the home. Once a spirit crosses into the light, there is no reason to return unless someone does something which pulls them back into the house, but that usually isn't the case. I was fairly certain, without even discussing it with Virginia, that the negative attachment sent to Gus was the culprit. Based on Virginia's feeling that this sinister presence had left while we were conducting the cleansing of the home, we had only hoped that our work was successful in removing the entity, but we had no way of confirming this on that night. Activity had stopped in the home, so we were hopeful that nothing more would bother the family, but at the same time, it was one of those cases where we knew we'd be getting the call back and the investigation would continue. Although we work on cases as long as needed, we are always hopeful, for the clients' sake, that we can stop the activity on our first visit. This would not be the case for the Upper Darby house.

I was again contacted by Sharan a day or two after receiving her email. She told me that Gus had experienced a frightening incident in the kitchen the night after the kitchen cabinet incident. Gus was alone in the kitchen, leaning over the sink getting a glass of water when suddenly, he felt something touch the right side of his neck and shoulder. Gus turned quickly to his right and saw a smoky figure in front of him. Gus panicked for a second but managed to open up his flip phone and snap a picture of the object as it moved away. Sharan said that figure in the picture looked like the shadow of a man wearing a hat and it was standing between their refrigerator and the door to the basement stairs. Sharan explained Gus' frightened reaction and stated that this was the first time he had been touched by the entity.

This is the picture that Gus took in the kitchen, right after he saw the smoky figure standing in front of him. Gus reported the figure walked right through the refrigerator. In this picture, you can see the figure on the wall between the refrigerator and the basement door. Part of the shadow figure appears to be on the top, middle part of the refrigerator, as well as partially on the white paper hanging on the side of the refrigerator. The figure has been reported by some to look like it is wearing a hat, and therefore, was referred to as the "Hat Man." It is also much more solid in the picture than Gus reported seeing it.

Attachments can be extremely complicated to deal with. Not only are we, as a resolution team, dealing with an entity that is not part of the physical world, but we have to work with the living person to which the entity is attached. As I have commented in earlier chapters, an interconnected energy always exists between the two. Certain circumstances may keep an attachment with a person, and this is often where "paranormal resolutionists" sometimes become spiritual counselors as they try

to work their way through the emotional, psychologi-
cal and physiological makeup of the person involved. I
highly depend on Virginia to connect with higher powers to give insight on what may be occurring between
the living and the dead. With information from her
"team" on the other side, we can then look at different
possibilities for moving forward and the proper course
to take. So after receiving Sharan's email, a phone call to
Virginia was in order.

It has become routine for Virginia and me to contin-
ually talk over cases for months after investigations, just
to make sure everything is still going well for the clients.
If there are any unresolved issues, we discuss those and
offer additional recommendations to families. As an
outside resource called in to help people, we can only do
so much. People going through supernatural experiences must also do a certain amount on their part to make
sure positive energy continues in a home. Sometimes
that means doing simple things like letting more sun-
light into a home, playing uplifting or relaxing music,
saging the house, or simply playing games and having
fun as a family. Other times, major life changes may be
necessary in order to facilitate the total resolution of a
haunting. A vast number of factors affect the outcome of
cases, and sometimes trial and error are the only course
to take until the situation is resolved. After extensively
speaking with Virginia about this haunting, her strong
psychic sense revealed that the negative attachment sent
to Gus had never really left!

During our phone call, Virginia "tuned in" on the
home and started receiving psychic impressions about
events happening there. She felt that the same evil entity that choked her was now present in a much stronger
way. Virginia commented, much like on the night of
our first visit to the home, that the spirit of the "angry

woman" who was the dominant energy in the home had such a powerful presence that she had kept this entity at bay. Now that she was gone, Virginia felt the negative entity coming in with a stronger ability and desire to wreak havoc in the home. Although the entity had "disappeared" for several weeks with no appearances, I now believe from similar past experiences that after Virginia and I conducted an energetic cleansing of the house, the vibrational state of the space in which we were working had changed. That is what a cleansing is meant to do after all. In this case, the cleansing altered the "frequency" of the space, and even though the entity was still present, it was not on the same frequency. So, in effect, it was not able to interact with the environment as it had before. This negative being likely did not like the way the energy now felt and may have stayed away just because of that. Essentially, the higher vibrational state in the home repelled it. When we talked with Gus and Sharan at the conclusion of our investigation, we informed them that we felt the house was clear of any ghosts. That information in itself can shift consciousness as thoughts and beliefs change about the situation. In turn, the vibrational state of the individual will shift to a higher level as well. When that happened, Gus himself was able to repel this entity. He just didn't know it. This is one of the reasons we give recommendations to families to complete extra work after we do a cleansing. It helps keep positive energy levels up in the house, as Virginia puts it.

As time went on after our first investigation, life happened within Sharan's and Gus' family with typical ups and downs. But over the course of several weeks, the vibrational state was slowly starting to come down to a lower level within the house and within Gus until the negative entity realigned with Gus' vibrational state.

From the family's perspective, the entity was back. It is important to recognize, though, that this entity was sent specifically to Gus through methods that aligned it with his energy. As long as it was still attached to Gus and their energy was in alignment, it could use that period of alignment to act out and be most effective. That's why we often see cycles of active periods and quiet periods with attachments. The vibrational state, or frequency of a person, plays a role in how outside energies affect them. When people feel great and are in a good physical and mental state, things seem to get quiet. When they become depressed, angry, or unwell, energy levels are down, so is their guard, and things start to happen.

After I spoke with Virginia and received confirmation that she felt the negative attachment was again active in the house, I contacted Sharan to find out exactly what was going on. Sharan reported that things were quiet right up until this point, but activity had started again in a way that they couldn't ignore, referring to the kitchen cabinet doors and drawers being pulled open and Gus being touched by this entity now referred to as the "Hat Man." I advised Sharan that we would continue to work with them and asked if she had followed through on some of the cleansing techniques that Virginia recommended for her to do after our visit. Sharan had been extremely busy, only able to complete a minimal amount of cleansing work. At this point, I wanted Virginia to speak directly with Sharan to get a better read on the house and determine a new course of action. I relayed to Sharan that Virginia would get in touch with her within the next few days, and we would determine our plan following their phone call. Virginia and Sharan spoke on and off for a few days, and Sharan did some saging in the house. All was quiet for now!

On May 16, 2010, Virginia and I received the following email from Sharan:

> Hi Mark and Virginia,
>
> Just to let you know, the change throwing has started again and last night our hallway light would not work. We kept switching it on/off from downstairs, but it would not come on. Gus went upstairs and turned on the bathroom light, and then he saw an arm come out of my son's room (a black, smoky, shadowy arm) and the hand reached to turn on the hallway light, and guess what? It works!!!!! Needless to say, he ran downstairs, white as a ghost, LOL, and told me what happened. I told Gus that he was just trying to be helpful!
>
> So, it was quiet for a while and now we will see what happens. I will say that this is the longest period that we've had without a lot of activity.
>
> Thanks,
> Sharan

This email from Sharan confirmed a few things. The saging and other energy work proved helpful to some extent. The family had enjoyed a long period with little activity. The description of the arm reaching out of Gus' son's room was much like the shadow figure we captured on the video camera in that same area. Rather than another ghost in the house, this was likely the same negative entity that had been sent to Gus. It was great to see that Sharan was trying to look on the positive side, adding a little humor to the situation despite the fact that this thing was still residing in their house.

With this new information, Virginia once again encouraged Sharan to persevere in her energy cleansing around the house, and Virginia was going to perform remote psychic and prayer work from home, having her group of mediums in New York also enact remote work to help stop the activity. Virginia hoped that a group effort might be more effective. Sharan reported that the activity seemed to slow down after Virginia and her psychic friends had performed their remote work. Things were quiet for over six months. But that period of non-activity ended, and Virginia and I got another email from Sharan on July 24, 2010.

Hi Virginia and Mark,

Virginia, the entity must have been looking over my shoulder last night when I emailed you and told you things were quiet. Activity started again!

I know what you are going to say, and I have been a little lax as we have been busy, but I will start the spritzing, smudging, and prayers again.

Gus heard footsteps stomping up and down the basement steps last week while I was upstairs with the little one.

Last night, the baby's bassinet (the one in the girls' room) was moved from along the wall, to in front of the doorway. I also had the pencil holder thrown at me while I was on the computer last night.

Today, at least 4 different times, the air conditioner turned on, again in the girls' room, while the door was wide open — both of the girls are at a friend's house today for a sleepover, and it doesn't have a remote.

Gus, our son and I, went out for a couple of hours and got home around 9:00 pm to find the downstairs playpen right in front of the doorway, and we go upstairs to find the girls room air conditioner on again. I told my son to unplug it.

It was almost nil for a pretty long time—I guess we will see what happens!

Take care,
Sharan

This latest email prompted great concern. The activity had thoroughly escalated since we last talked with Sharan. Although she had been somewhat lax in fulfilling the energy work in the house, this alarming amount of activity worried us. Virginia reminded me that this entity was the only "spirit" in the house now, and when the conditions were right, it acted out with much more aggression than when held back by the spirit of the dominant woman. Virginia told me she would weigh some options, would contact Sharan, then get back to me to discuss a game plan.

Several days passed before I heard back from Virginia. When we finally spoke, she said that Sharan and Gus were planning a trip to Italy in a few months. After discussing the trip with a few of her psychic colleagues, they felt that a long trip over a massive body of water might break the attachment to Gus. Virginia contacted Sharan and spoke to her about this theory. Virginia recommended that Sharan keep doing the smudging and prayer work in her home,then wait and see if the trip would break the connection between Gus and the Hat Man. If that proved successful, we would not have to do any additional work, and the case would finally be resolved. Sharan and Gus agreed to wait and see what happened after the trip and then go from there.

Sharan and Gus left for their trip in late October, but up until their departure, there were periods of high activity and periods of little to no activity. The family was to be away for nearly two months, so we were very hopeful that things would be resolved when they returned. Unfortunately, that would not be the case!

The following is a portion of another email that Virginia received from Sharan on December 14, 2010. This was in response to an email that Virginia sent to Sharan, checking on the welfare of the family a few days after their return from Italy. Some personal information has been removed from the email:

Hi Virginia!

We are back from Italy!

Today, the oven was on and neither of us turned it on. I had left to pick up the kids. Gus called me and asked if I was trying to kill him and the kids cause he smelled something burning. I made pizza dough, wrapped it in plastic, put it in the oven to rise and the oven was on burning the plastic.

Then, Gus hears our daughter upstairs talking. He goes up 3 times and she's asleep soundly each time. But he swears it's her voice. So, we will see what happens.

Have a fabulous Holiday!
Sharan

Obviously, we were disappointed to hear that the trip had not severed the connection between Gus and the Hat Man. The best-case scenario would have been a broken connection with the entity leaving on its own. Gus reported that he did not experience any activity while in Italy. Virginia's associates appeared to be partially correct in their theory that the Hat Man would not follow Gus across the ocean. The next question was, where do we go from here?

Because it was now the Christmas and New Year holiday season, Virginia and I asked Sharan to keep working on spiritually cleansing the house. This seemed to be effective when it was done consistently. While Virginia wanted to research more strategies which would not be too stressful for Gus, she did not rule out the possibility of enacting more extreme metaphysical work with Gus, but again, she did not want to push the boundaries with his existing heart issue. Keeping the Hat Man at bay had proved to be an arduous task, and our end goal was to completely resolve the issue so that we could alleviate Sharan's role of constant energy cleansing. Sharan agreed to this course of action for the time being, and we asked her to let us know how things were going after the new year.

Things seemed to have gone well through the holidays, but on January 17, 2011, I received the following email update from Sharan:

Hi Mark,

Just wanted to let you know that things aren't bad, but definitely have started up again and I have been doing the prayers and holy water.

Today, I told the kids to help me get the laundry sorted and my son opened the basement door to find things neatly placed in the doorway.

Things and money have been disappearing and moving.

My daughter saw something/someone a few days ago, go into the girls room — she asked Gus, "Who is that?"

We also have been hearing footsteps, voices, meowing, and other unaccountable noises constantly.

I'm just keeping you aware. I will say that there has been a lot of tension in the home, and Gus has really been stressed and is very vocal about it, and I think it's feeding off the negative energy. When I told Gus about maybe calming down, he got really agitated with me.

Sharan

Obviously, a return to Upper Darby was imminent. With so many children in the house, the profusion of activity was not emotionally healthy for any of them. Not to mention, much stress had compounded the relationship between Sharan and Gus. Although the activity had diminished in frequency, the occasional activity was wearing the family down. I spoke with Virginia, and we agreed to return to the property and see what we could do in-person. The PPA had become immensely busy at this time, and several cases had been scheduled. We planned to return to Upper Darby in April, and Virginia promised Sharan that she would keep in touch with her until our return. Unfortunately, activity seemed to be increasing as we got closer to April.

Below is an email from Sharon on March 1, 2011, updating us on the activity and inquiring when we would return. By her tone, you can tell that Sharan was getting anxious for our return:

Hi Virginia and Mark,

Virginia, I think I remember you saying you all might come up on a Wednesday, during the day. I'm just wondering if you have figured out when. The activity is still occurring, a lot!

The baby's bottle got thrown against the front door today and broke the bottle, this thing growls at us, the chandelier and pots shake like crazy, items get thrown from shelves, and this is only the last two days.

Thank you!
Sharan

Unfortunately, we were still a month away before we could get to Sharan and Gus. Trying to quickly work through our pending cases, we received a deluge of requests for help and were having a hard time keeping up. Most clients were reporting severe activity, so we couldn't put any of them on the back burner. This case, once again, was becoming one of those urgent cases. Based on the latest update from Sharan, the activity was reaching an uncomfortable level, and we didn't want anyone getting hurt. We scheduled a date for the first Wednesday in April, which was the earliest we could go. We hoped that the family would hold on for another four or five weeks. Time would tell if we would experience similar activity as we did on our first visit, and by Sharan's accounts, the odds were good. When the day finally arrived, those odds became reality!

Chapter 7

A Day to Remember

It was a year to the week since our first investigation at the Upper Darby house. During that time, periods of extreme physical activity unfolded, then stretches of none. Some activity concerned the family, while other incidents were purely annoying. By the time we were able to return to the home, the activity had returned to the same level as when Sharan first contacted us, if not worse. The activity, however, was different! Virginia and I decided it was time perform another physical investigation to make sure the same persistent issue existed, not something new that could have been brought in by someone. This investigation would have to be somewhat different. Since we knew there was an attachment to Gus, we wanted him and Sharan to leave as our investigation started so we could focus more on the house. This was the first time we had encountered a case where the physical activity had returned as strongly as it had been before a cleansing. It was also the first time we had tried so many different ways to help a family without success. Because there were five children in the home, we felt the least disruptive way to investigate would be to go during the week when most of the kids were in school, and it would also afford us the opportunity to investigate during the day. Sharan told us that the activity was also occurring frequently during daylight hours, so we wanted to compare that with our findings from the initial night investigation.

On Wednesday, April 6, 2011, we arrived back at the house at 11:30 a.m. for a second physical investigation. This time the team consisted of Virginia, Paul, and me. Bob was not available because of his work schedule. This investigation would not be comprehensive like the first visit, it would be more of a fact-finding mission, but we did want to document any physical activity, should any occur. We also wanted to try and duplicate the "Hat Man" photo that Gus had shared with us.

Greeted by Gus and Sharan and after receiving the latest update of occurrences from the previous week, Paul and I began to investigate the shadow figure that appeared in the photo. Virginia was talking with Gus and Sharan at that time, so Paul and I made our way to the kitchen with my camera. Gus followed shortly behind, and when he entered the kitchen, I asked him to show us where he was and what he was doing when he witnessed the figure. Gus explained that he was standing at the sink getting a glass of water when he felt something touch the right side of his neck and shoulder. He turned quickly to the right and observed the "Hat Man" standing in front of him. Gus stated that it moved across the kitchen and went right through the refrigerator, moving towards the basement door. Gus initially froze when he saw it but somehow mustered the courage and foresight to take the picture. Armed with this information, I started moving around the kitchen with my camera and a flashlight in an attempt to recreate the shadow. Since Gus had seen this figure at night, it was possible that outside lights had created a shadow from something in the kitchen. No matter where I went or how I illuminated the light, I couldn't get any type of shadow to materialize. Gus had also observed the figure moving on that night, which complicated our efforts. Trying to duplicate the shadow in the photo and to recreate a realistic moving shadow in the kitchen proved impossible. As I worked my way around the kitchen trying a variety of techniques, I heard Gus talking to Paul in the dining room. Gus had become upset and angry with me. I could hear him inquiring why I would dismiss his photo, and he asked Paul directly, "Why doesn't he believe me?" Paul told Gus that we believed him, but this was something we had to perform on every case with every piece of potential evidence, even with photos that we take ourselves. Paul explained that this process helps us find the actual cause that may have not been immediately apparent, or it helps to confirm that it is authentic. Paul also assured Gus that we had experienced too much ourselves not to believe him, and Gus appeared to be understanding of that. My intentions were certainly not to upset Gus, but as I explained to him at the time, we look at every little piece of information objectively to see where it leads us.

Unable to dismiss the figure in the photo as having a natural cause, I told Virginia and Paul that I could not recreate it in any way. Virginia laughed at me and said, "I told you so!" On a psychic level, she had already verified the figure in the photo was the entity attached to Gus. She didn't need any physical proof to clarify. However, the non-psychic people in the room needed to gain insight in other ways. I have experience with showing Virginia various clients' pictures which contain anomalies in the shots, and Virginia has been extremely accurate at tuning into the energy of a space just through the photo and describing to me who she feels is there. Unless the anomaly is not a ghost, however, she just tells me that it's not a ghost. We have been repeatedly able to confirm information that Virginia receives through pictures, so between her confidence that what Gus captured in his photo was an entity, and the fact that I could not get any kind of similar shadow to appear in the kitchen, I was satisfied that the figure was likely this negative entity. And if you remember back to the first investigation, the shadow that we captured on the video camera entering the son's room was consistent with the shape, makeup, and color of what Gus had captured in his photo. When we showed the video to Virginia during our review, the first thing she said was "that's him!" referring to the "Hat Man." Continuing with the conversation about the Hat Man in the dining room, which now included Gus, Paul, Sharan, Virginia and me, we talked about Virginia's initial impression that this shadow figure was a masculine energy. She felt it was not a demon but a human based soul, just twisted and morphed into this negative, dark, shadow-like entity. Virginia sensed that its only purpose was to disrupt and ruin Gus' life.

The time had come, and we were ready to conduct our second investigation. As I mentioned earlier, this was going to be a condensed investigation and not a full-blown comprehensive investigation. We brought much of the same technical equipment but did not set up the stationary cameras nor the stationary audio recorders. We were mainly working with handheld gear but did leave one recorder running in the attic's front room and one recorder in the basement. Gus and Sharan packed-up their infant and were headed out for a couple hours to give us some time to work. I told them that we would call when ready for their return. Gus and Sharan left the house and we were on our own.

Virginia wanted to meditate in the dining room to see if she could receive guidance on activity happening there. Paul and I were eager to sit in the attic for a few minutes to try and capture any EVP's on our audio or video recorders. EVP stands for Electronic Voice Phenomenon, and the theory behind this technique involves investigators asking questions and trying to get a "phantom voice" recorded on an audio recorder. Any voice that appears on the recording that wasn't audible to those present at the time it was recorded, is the EVP. Paul and I decided to sit in the front attic room. Paul sat on a chair and I on the floor. Within just a few minutes of entering and sitting down, I unexpectedly witnessed a quarter go flying through the air in the room across the hall, hitting the wall with a ping. I immediately jumped up, bolted down the stairs to the second floor, and feverishly looked through all the rooms. No one was there. I attempted to locate anyone in the house who may have thrown the coin. Even though I had observed quarters being thrown on our video from the first investigation, I still thought someone could be in the house throwing quarters. It just seemed too convenient to happen as soon as we sat down. I asked Virginia if anyone had come into the house, and she said no. Virginia stated she was still in the same position as when we went upstairs, and she was the only one present on the first floor. I walked back up the stairs from the master bedroom to the attic rooms, and as I ascended the stairs, I noticed they were very creaky. It was impossible that someone could have thrown a coin into the back room and run down the stairs without being heard or seen. Besides that, I observed the coin fly from my left to right, which was moving in the direction of the stairs, so the coin had to be thrown from within that room. If someone had been on the stairs, I would have caught him. I went into the back room, found the quarter on the floor, picked it up and felt that is was warm to the touch. I noted the date, but it appeared there was no consistency with the dates of any of the prior quarters, so we didn't find any specific meaning associated with the quarters at this point. I still wasn't satisfied that Paul, Virginia and I were the only occupants in house, so I took one extra step and opened a crawl space door located at the end of the room where the coin would have been thrown from. My heart pounded as I opened the door, half expecting to find someone there. But when I opened it, nothing appeared. I was relieved, amazed, and elated to discover that no one appeared in the crawl space, but I was also thrilled to have experienced a phenomenal first-hand, personal experience. I happened to be in the right place at the right time, for once, and observed the quarter flying across the room. Paul's video camera, of course, was pointing in the other direction!

When I concluded my investigation of the flying quarter, Paul and I went downstairs and met with Virginia. She was still picking up on the Hat Man and felt that it was much more present than on the night of our first visit. This was good news in one respect because we were now certain it was the same entity causing the issues and not something new that we had to deal with. Virginia wanted to check the basement next because Sharan had told us that their wine bottles had recently been pulled off a shelf and smashed on the concrete floor.

After a few minutes walking around the basement, Virginia became conscious of a male spirit not previously present. This was not news I wanted to hear. Virginia sensed that while the homeowners were in Italy, Gus had come into contact with this ghost while working on their property. Virginia perceived it was a Nazi soldier that had attacked Gus, as if he were still fighting the war in Italy; she also sensed that this spirit attached to Gus and accompanied him back to his Upper Darby residence. Virginia believed that the soldier did not know how to break the connection with Gus and further concluded that the soldier was enraged and volatile. Gus later confirmed that while visiting their property in Italy, he was indeed tilling the land. Gus was aware of a few historical facts about the property that he later informed us about. Ten German soldiers had perished during World War II and were still buried somewhere on the property. Ironically, Virginia believed the soldiers would have been there guarding a cache of buried money. Gus confirmed that they occasionally found coins while digging in the yard. The synchronicity of Gus' life experiences certainly intrigued us, and coins seemed to be a major theme. I asked Virginia about the original soldier she had sensed in the basement, but she was not feeling him there anymore. She had only caught one glimpse, and he never returned.

Virginia, Paul and I also spent time trying to determine the cause of smashed imported wine bottles. We also tried to coax the spirit to repeat the incident but to no avail. Virginia sensed that it was the German soldier breaking the bottles. He was angry and confused about being pulled into this strange situation, and because of this, was smashing the wine bottles to take it out on Gus.

After fifteen or twenty minutes with no activity, Virginia wanted to try a "little experiment" and retrieved a CD player and a CD of the Hail Mary prayer from her car. She would play the prayer on a repeat cycle to see what happened. Virginia stayed in the basement to start the recording while Paul and I went to the second floor. Just before leaving the basement, Paul said, "I'm going to leave my video camera here." Paul placed his camera on a bench at the far end of the basement and pointed it in the direction of the stairs where Virginia was setting up the CD player. Later, we were extremely grateful for Paul's decision.

Ascending the stairs to the second floor, Paul and I turned to the left and walked the opposite direction down the hallway to get to the master bedroom. As Paul and I walked into the bedroom, I closed the door to limit the amount of noise. Virginia tends to become very loud on occasion, and we didn't want her voice showing up on the audio recorder we would be using. I left the door ajar about two to three inches, just enough to see if anybody walked down the hallway. I sat on the bed to the right of the bedroom door with Paul standing to the left of the door facing me. Frequently, Paul and I engage in random conversation, intentionally ignoring spirits to get them to work for our attention. Tonight, our plan seemed to pay off. As I sat on the bed talking to Paul, the bedroom door opened about two feet and quickly shut. I looked at Paul. Paul looked at me, and I just shrugged my shoulders, stood up, and opened the door. I first thought that somebody must have opened another door in the house, creating a suction of air to open and then pull the door shut. As I opened the door to investigate, right in front of me, lined up horizontally across the floor, four quarters were placed that had not been there five minutes ago. Instantly, I knew that air pressure did not move the door. In a sarcastic tone, I asked Paul if this ghost were a magician, but part of me was sincere in this thought. "Why the heck were coins spontaneously appearing out of nowhere?" This strange incident had us standing there laughing while shaking our heads. But the story gets even stranger!

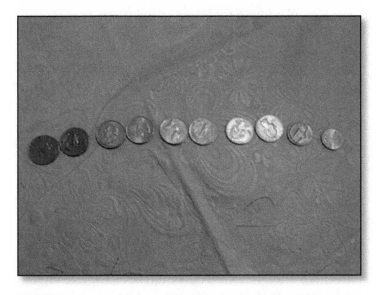

The family reported finding this line of coins in the dining room, similar to the line of coins that Mark and Paul found in the master bedroom doorway during the second investigation.

Paul and I went back into the bedroom and pressed whoever was with us to open the door again. Nothing happened! We asked for a coin to appear. Nothing happened! We even tried to capture a voice on our audio recorder, but we wouldn't know if that was successful until we later reviewed the recording. About ten minutes past and we heard Virginia yelling for us from the first floor, asking us to come down.

We hurried downstairs and told Virginia about our experience in the master bedroom. Virginia said, "You're not going to believe this, but I just had a quarter fall out of thin air in the basement."

"You're kidding!" I replied.

Virginia asked us to accompany her to the basement where she had been walking around with the Hail Mary recording playing in the background when a quarter fell out of thin air right behind her, loudly pinging on the concrete floor. Because of Paul's instinct in leaving his video camera recording in the basement, we caught it on camera! Initially, we thought that perhaps a quarter had been loosely sitting on a rafter or was tucked away on the basement ceiling when it had come loose and fallen by coincidence, but we searched the entire ceiling and couldn't find any additional coins. We also canvassed for any holes or vents in the ceiling where someone could have dropped a quarter, but there were none. Not finding anything in the basement, I went upstairs to the living room above the spot where the quarter had fallen. I wanted to check for any holes or vents that might be more visible from the top side, but the living room had wall to wall carpeting and no holes of any kind. It seemed we had been gifted another quarter! The running joke at this point was why couldn't it be hundred-dollar bills instead of quarters. It would at least make the aggravation worth it for the family.

Virginia is present in the basement when a quarter spontaneously falls out of the ceiling area onto the concrete floor during the second investigation. The two pictures presented were taken from Paul's video camera which he left in the basement.

The falling coin can be seen in this picture, as indicated by the circle. You can see in the first picture that the coin is not present.

Once we thoroughly checked the basement ceiling, Paul asked if he could spend some time there by himself, so Virginia and I headed up to the second floor to do additional investigating. Paul sat quietly in a chair with not much happening and decided to start asking questions with his audio recorder running. Paul also wanted to try and replicate the falling coin experience that Virginia had earlier witnessed. He started asking anyone who may be in the basement to make a coin fall from the ceiling. After a few unsuccessful attempts to get a quarter to appear, Paul commented, "I'm here by myself. There is nothing you need to fear from me. I'm just a big Polack!" and right then, a quarter fell from the ceiling. Obviously, Paul was surprised and logged the time on his recorder at 3:41 p.m. Paul then tried to get another quarter to fall, but apparently it was just a one quarter per person kind of deal. This time we were certain of no quarters hidden anywhere on the ceiling. Thanks to Paul's video camera, we also captured the second quarter falling. And on a side note, Paul is of Polish descent if you didn't happen to catch that or know what a Polack is!

Paul looks at the ceiling where the second quarter fell.

While Paul was doing his work in the basement, Virginia and I went to the master bedroom. Virginia sat down on the attic stairs and closed her eyes while she "tuned-in" on the space to see if she felt anything. After giving historical impressions of the block and surrounding area, Virginia turned and said, "He's here!" referring to the Hat Man. He was standing in the hallway just outside the door. I walked over and, of course, didn't see anything, but my hair stood up on my arms, and I felt a tingle in my spine. I'm not sure if my sensations were caused by energy or the knowledge that it was there, but I had the chills. Virginia warned me that the Hat Man was in an aggressive, challenging posture. He felt the energy from my law enforcement background and saw me as a threat. Not backing down from a challenge, I told the Hat Man that I wasn't afraid of him, that he could do nothing to me. Virginia told me to be careful because this thing was going to knock me on my ass, but I stood my ground and commented that if it possessed so much power, to show me something physical, such as slamming the door in my face. Virginia conveyed that the Hat Man's response was that it did not need to prove itself to me. At that point I knew it was no issue for me, or I would have already been attacked. I did not believe that it could hurt me unless I gave it the power to do so. Inflicting fear was its biggest source of power, and fear was something it would not provoke in me. I told the Hat Man that it was just a pawn of someone else's bidding and thanked it for the lessons that it was teaching us. I said we were going to make its existence in the home as intolerable as possible, but we were first going to give it the option of being in control of its destiny to make the decision to leave on its own. The Hat Man didn't leave the house at that time, however, my words totally disarmed it of any ability to affect me, and it left our presence. In my experience, approaching a negative entity with the feeling that you are "of the light" and speaking intelligently and firmly, much like talking to a disobedient child, usually disarms the situation and removes any influence. One must approach an entity with the understanding that the entity is what it is, no more, no less. It fulfills its own purpose in the universe, but it certainly does not have any control if a person does not surrender to it. In this case, my approach worked! Someday I may find myself knocked on my ass, but until then, I'll continue to fill myself with light and stand my ground against evil! Although I was talking to an empty hallway, from my perspective, I believed that I had disarmed the Hat Man for now!

Paul summoned Virginia and me to the first floor to inform us about another coin falling from the ceiling, and we discussed the other six quarters observed throughout the day. The quarters bore different years, yet we still couldn't find a relevant pattern. Virginia sensed that the entity had the intention to corrupt Gus financially and that the quarters thrown around the house were definitely caused by this evil entity. The quarters served as a constant reminder that the Hat Man was still there, sticking it right in Gus' face, in a manner of speaking. According to Virginia, the quarters were a symbolic representation of money in general.

Based on the investigation that day, activity was quite obviously still occurring at the Upper Darby home. We documented a higher than usual amount of activity than on most cases and had an equally abnormal amount of personal experiences. We spent copious amounts of time trying to establish the cause and origin of the quarters appearing out of thin air and also how the bedroom door opened and closed by itself. No natural causes for any activity could be determined, and when we added all our experiences and evidence together, it was obvious that this was a poltergeist case.

A poltergeist, as described by Wikipedia — In ghostlore, a poltergeist (/ˈpoʊltərˌɡaɪst/; German for "noisy ghost" or "noisy spirit") is a type of ghost or spirit that is responsible for physical disturbances, such as loud noises and objects being moved or destroyed. They are purportedly capable of pinching, biting, hitting, and tripping people. Most accounts of poltergeists describe the movement or levitation of objects such as furniture and cutlery, or noises such as knocking on doors.

We had now completed two physical investigations, and on both dates, we experienced a higher than average amount of activity. Quarters were being thrown, quarters were falling out of thin air, and quarters were being lined up in a straight little line on the floor. Toys were turning on, video cameras were turning off, and doors were opening and closing by themselves. To top it off, Virginia had been choked, and Bob felt like someone tried to push him over during the first investigation. If this didn't fit the definition of a poltergeist, I didn't know what did, and these were just a few events we were observing. The family was experiencing this activity on a daily basis, and I could see why they were at the breaking point. Unlike a normal haunting where one ghost acts with poltergeist type behavior, we had many acting that way. Over the course of two investigations, we concluded that four prominent spirits of varying natures existed in this home, and all four were remarkably adept at creating physical happenings. Most often ghosts cannot manipulate physical objects. Witnesses typically report seeing figures or shadows, hearing sounds, or even getting strange feelings, but most ghosts, I suspect, cannot move things. It was very rare to find four spirits in one place that could interact physically at this level: the angry woman, her son, the German soldier, and the Hat Man. All had inflicted a profusion of chaos over time, in their own particular way. From an investigator's perspective, it was an amazing experience.

I often get asked why we investigate in the dark or at night. The main reason is our clients typically report the most amount of activity occurring later in the day or at night. If we intend on using the infrared function on our cameras, we must have the lights out and it has to be dark. The infrared feature does not work in normal lighting, so the lights have to be off to take advantage of the infrared light spectrum. And frankly, it is the most convenient time of the day for us to investigate with our busy family lives. But we also investigate during the day. This particular investigation started in the morning, progressed into mid-day, and we captured some of our best evidence and had some amazing personal experiences. It really just depends on when the activity happens the most, and when we are available to go, that determines what time of day we investigate. I was thrilled we decided to conduct our second investigation during the day.

Towards the end of this visit, Virginia was able to remove the German soldier from the house. He was a surprise for us, but he wanted out, so we did not have any issues with him. Virginia felt that this soldier was only causing a small portion of the activity, but more than anything else, Gus had been negatively affected by its energy, thus causing exhaustion, irritability, and anger. Virginia, Paul and I discussed our next steps for removing the Hat Man from the house, and Virginia knew this would require the assistance of additional associates.

Virginia wanted to return to the house on a different date with her whole "team" of metaphysical workers, an incredible group of support people whom we call upon when a case requires the efforts of several psychic mediums and energy workers. These psychics help deal with particular issues more difficult or dangerous than our typical cases. They are also Virginia's closest friends. I am able to say that they are now very good friends of mine as well. Jack, a psychic medium, has an extensive background and working knowledge of Voodoo. He has worked with our team on many occasions, so it was important to have him accompany us. Virginia's husband Chris, and their friend, Camille, would also aid Virginia should we make a return trip to the Upper Darby House to complete our work.

When Gus and Sharan returned to the house, we updated them on our findings and told them about our continuing experiences with the quarters. They found the events interesting but were not surprised. We informed them of the German soldier that Virginia located in the basement, and she explained to Gus that he should feel more energetic and less irritable now that the soldier had departed. Gus confirmed Virginia's historical information regarding the German soldiers on the family's property in Italy. We explained that the Hat Man was still strongly attached to Gus and we would soon be providing some recommendations on some things that we felt Gus needed to do on his part to help alleviate the situation. We also recommended having our full metaphysical team come in to try to disconnect this attachment from Gus using several different strategies. Gus and Sharan agreed to have us back, and we scheduled another visit for the upcoming Sunday.

Although we were unsuccessful at resolving the entire haunting on our second visit, we did manage to remove one more pesky spirit, offering a little relief to Gus until we could get rid of the main issue. During our visit in the home, we had a few incredible experiences that left us scratching our heads. Even Virginia, who sees and feels spirits on a daily basis only sometimes encounters physical activity, but when she does, it is never to this extent. This was definitely a day to remember!

Chapter 8

Review & Revisit

Because our second investigation ended early, I had an opportunity to go to bed fairly early that evening. After an investigation where people encounter amazing experiences with the supernatural, good or bad, investigators tend to replay those events as they lie down to sleep. At least I do! I kept thinking of all the instances that our members had quarters appearing out of thin air. The more I thought about the situation, the more realistic it became that this activity resulted from one of the entities in the house. Virginia was certain it was the Hat Man, and as I stated before, she has always been accurate with her information. I had no reason to doubt her now. I was ecstatic that we captured so much activity during our limited time there. Having investigated for only a little over twelve hours, over two different days a year apart, did not constitute a large amount of time in which to document activity, but document we did! I actually had the urge to get out of bed and start reviewing our recordings right then, but I knew it was in my best interest to sleep.

The next morning was rough though, because I was eager to start the review but had to go to work. The consolation was, two of my trooper colleagues I would be working with that morning were on our team and I would be able to fill them in on all they missed. They were certainly disappointed to hear about missing out on so much activity. Most of our cases are usually quiet with only small occurrences. So, the Upper Darby case was indeed rare. Working with people who have objective, inquiring minds is a bonus, and I can always receive additional feedback as I relate various situations to them. Getting multiple opinions on physical events is helpful and adds valuable feedback. Throughout the years, we added skeptics to our team, and skeptics often give us the best reasons as to why things happen. Skeptics look at things differently than the rest of us. Many times, skeptics are the people who help validate paranormal evidence when all they can do is shrug their shoulders and admit they have no idea how something occurred.

The review of the second investigation would be quicker because we only had to review two voice recorders and two video cameras. After speaking with Virginia, we decided that Paul and I would work on the review, while she would return to the Upper Darby house to make another attempt at ridding the home of the Hat Man with her group of mediums. Virginia, her husband Chris, Jack, and Camille would go. Chris has the ability to relax into a deep meditative state and go through a home by a type of mental projection. Jack and Camille are extremely gifted psychic mediums who gather information in various ways. Jack is also a medical intuitive, and one of our goals was to have him work with Gus to determine underlying issues which might be manifesting the Hat Man to him in specific ways. Camille worked with crystals and stones as applied to vibrational states of people and places. We asked for

Camille's assessment and recommendations for the family so they could use the stones to help elevate the home's low vibrational state.

Virginia and her spiritual group went to the Upper Darby home on the Sunday following our second investigation. Before taking any action, Virginia asked Camille to do a walk-through of the home to pick up on the relevant "hot spots." Camille was the only one in the group without any knowledge of events in the home. Virginia had already discussed certain information with Chris and Jack, so she wanted a fresh set of psychic eyes to take a look at the property. During the walk-through, Sharan was present with Camille and Virginia. Camille sensed activity in the same areas where Virginia had experienced activity, and Sharan confirmed this. Those rooms included the basement, the son's room, the master bedroom and the attic. Camille reported that she sensed activity throughout the house but most prominently in those four areas. While in the master bedroom, Sharan alarmingly stated that she was being scratched on her upper left arm. Sharan pulled up her shirt sleeve to reveal fresh scratches — not a good start to the visit.

After Jack met with Gus, he became worried about Gus' fragile state of health; specifically, Jack was worried about Gus' heart. Virginia's main concern was also Gus' condition, and if they were going to rid Gus of this entity, they did not want to exacerbate the situation. Jack was concerned that Gus might experience another heart attack if the Hat Man tried to fight the detachment. Sharan also revealed that Gus had experienced a minor stroke since our first investigation.

After discussing the situation, Virginia felt it best for Gus and Sharan to leave while they worked. Gus and Sharan removed themselves from the house, and the group began their cleansing. Rather than attempting to remove the attachment from Gus while he was present, the group wanted to work directly on the Hat Man itself. Virginia was not directly picking up on the entity's presence but felt it coming and going. The groups' intentions were most likely keeping it away.

Virginia uttered protective prayers for the group and called on her guides and angels to assist them. Collectively, the group used psychic visualization techniques often used on attachment cases and began cutting "cords" connecting Gus and the Hat Man. Many believe that when two people, or entities, come into contact, they are energetically connected. Cutting the cords provided a metaphysical technique to help break the energetic connection between the two. Next, Virginia did a binding technique on the Hat Man — again, a visualization method used to energetically put the entity in a type of "straight jacket." The goal was to contain it in an energy wrap so it could not reattach itself to Gus or to another person or spirit. Once completed, Virginia called on higher powers to remove the entity; she then articulated some closing prayers. Once the group had finished trying to remove the Hat Man, Virginia and Camille scoured the house with sage and crystals. They called Sharan and Gus back to the house and explained what had transpired. The only thing to do now was wait for and see the outcome.

When Virginia returned home, she immediately called me. Unpacking from the trip, she had opened up an old cigar box where she stores her oils. Used in the Upper Darby cleansing, Virginia excitedly explained that when she closed the box, it only contained her oils. When she returned home and opened it, two quarters were found in the box with the oils. Never putting any objects besides oils in her case, especially quarters, Virginia was positive they were not there before she left the Upper Darby house. Apparently, she had received a tip from the other side, but at fifty cents, that may have been an insult!

Back at PPA headquarters, Paul and I were finishing up our review of the recordings. Nothing new appeared on the voice recorders, but we were elated about video footage capturing the quarters that fell out of thin air. The coins can be seen falling and you can hear them ping off the floor. My favorite part was watching Virginia's reaction when the quarter fell. She quickly turned around and exclaimed in her Queens, NY accent, "Alright, that's it! Do it again!" If you remember, Virginia gets a little freaked out in basements, so I was thrilled to see that she stayed with the activity and asked for more. Paul sounded amazed when it happened to him but continued as well, logging the time and asking for a repeat! Many people are creeped out at being alone in dark spaces and flee if things start moving, but that is exactly when we should be present to document events when they happen. Knowing that investigators are scared doesn't exactly inspire confidence in clients and it is disheartening to me when I hear about investigators who run from activity with clients present. Virginia and Paul did a great job in documenting these events which provided more small pieces of evidence that we could add to the larger puzzle.

Rather than drive all the way back to Upper Darby, I decided to call Sharan and Gus to review the evidence. Virginia had already discussed her team's findings while at the house on Sunday. I emailed the video clips of the two quarters falling in the basement and advised Sharan and Gus that we did not have any additional physical evidence from our recorders. They were actually relieved that we had not experienced more activity. The first investigation yielded an overwhelming amount of recorded activity; the second investigation, much less but was very specific to the coin experiences. On a positive note, we made $1.75 with an additional fifty cents that Virginia found in her box of oils. In total, we pulled in two dollars and twenty-five cents on this case. Not much, but more than any other spirit has paid us for an investigation! It made sense that we had experienced less activity on the second visit, because there were fewer spirits in the home and Gus was not present during this investigation. Since Gus was the intended target of the Hat Man, there was no reason for the Hat Man to interact with us as he would with Gus. He most likely saw us a threat as we tried to remove him, so he had to exhibit some bravado to let us know he wasn't going anywhere. Unfortunately, this proved to be true, and we would soon return!

Chapter 9

The Final Visit

Although we were optimistic in the efficacy of our spiritual team, their efforts had not been as effective as we had hoped. The group had concerns when working with the Hat Man without Gus' presence. The fragile situation needed a delicate approach. The team did not want to cause further medical issues for Gus, and they certainly didn't want to instigate another stroke or heart attack.

Virginia had continued contact with Sharan over the next few weeks, and Sharan reported that the activity had calmed down since Virginia and her spiritual group had visited, but small things were still occurring. Virginia would continue to psychically work on the Upper Darby house from her New York home as this was shaping up to be one of the most persistent entities that we've had to deal with. One issue was that Gus did not want to take into consideration some of the recommendations that Virginia had offered him. One in particular, was to have Gus work with a very wise, and very spiritual priest that Virginia was friends with. The priest had offered to work with Gus, and Gus did come from a Catholic background, but because of personal reasons that I won't go into here, Gus did not want to work with him. I think largely because he had made many attempts to get a few different local priests to come in and they all blew him off after very long conversations. Gus seemed very frustrated with the church and didn't care to go through it all again to just be rejected one more time. Let me also make the distinction that although all priests are religious by the nature of their work, but not all priests have the same spiritual views of dealing with the paranormal or psychic phenomena. Virginia believed that her friend could very gently rid Gus of this entity without any physical issues, but Gus was not interested in going that route, and we respected his wishes. Virginia's spirit guides revealed that Gus' decision, in part, was influenced by the Hat Man, so essentially, the Hat Man was veering him away from clergy.

A couple months had passed since our last visit, and activity was occasionally occurring. Virginia communicated to Sharan that she was going to remotely try another "binding" ceremony on the Hat Man. This energetic technique involved Virginia writing her intentions and binding process on a piece of paper, and after a lengthy meditation on Gus, the property, and the Hat Man, she would then fold the paper around a card of St. Benedict and the Archangel Michael. Virginia would place the wrapped items in a small container of water, add specific incense and oils to the water, then freeze it into a solid block of ice with the paper and cards inside. (Note: This is a summarized version of what Virginia does and not the whole process, so we don't recommend people doing this at home and expecting results.) The intent of this technique is to bind the energy of the entity, causing less impact on the person to which it is attached. We hoped this binding would keep the entity at bay until another plan could be devised.

Several weeks passed, and the activity continued. The good news? It was restricted to Gus for the most part. Not that it was good news for Gus since he was the one having the interactions, but it helped alleviate much of the activity for the rest of the family. Unfortunately, Gus' mental and physical states were still being affected by the negative energy, so we had to do something. I had a connection with a white Voodoo church in Philadelphia, very close to where Gus lived. Voodoo is just Voodoo unless used for evil purposes. The stereotypical Voodoo shown on television is dark Voodoo, more dramatic with spells cast to cause harm to others, which makes for good television and movies. This church did not want to be lumped in with those stereotypes, so they advertised as a white Voodoo church. I contacted the priestess who runs the church and explained the situation. Although the Hat Man was sent to Gus by Santeria, the priestess told me that she was expertly equipped to handle attachments, no matter how they occurred. At the time, I wanted to fight fire with fire. If Santeria was the cause, then maybe Voodoo was the solution. As I stated in earlier chapters, Voodoo and Santeria share similar backgrounds, and the priestess said it didn't matter if Voodoo or Santeria were involved; she felt certain that she could take care of the situation without harm to Gus. I explained that Gus did not want to work with someone from his faith for personal reasons, but perhaps he would try something different. After I spoke with him, I would call her back to schedule a meeting. The priestess said that Gus would need to come to her church where she would perform the ceremony, and she also invited me to attend. I was intrigued to see how she worked if Gus should agree.

When I contacted Sharan and asked her to inform Gus about the Voodoo church, Gus was definitely not interested. I wasn't sure if it was the Hat Man's influence or if Gus felt the situation too bizarre. Furthermore, we were starting to run out of options. We could not get Gus to work with clergy, having an exorcism to remove the attachment may have caused a heart attack, and the level of activity likely decreased enough for him to tolerate it, although it was still affecting him. Luckily, the activity was presently not as impactful as it had been in the past. This brings me back to the point I made earlier, that it takes some work on the part of the person an entity is attached to, to help disconnect the issue. If someone truly doesn't want an attachment removed, whatever the reason, there is nothing we can do to remove it. This was not the case with Gus, but it was difficult to get him to try some of our recommendations that may have helped.

There was one last thing we wanted to try. Virginia wished to return to the property and try one more binding technique that would essentially attach the Hat Man to the ground in the backyard. His presence was significantly weaker since Virginia's last attempt, but her strategy had only reduced its affective energy, whereas this other technique would bind it outside of the home. In order to be effective, Virginia needed to be on the property, so we contacted Sharan and set up another date to return. On this trip, we brought my wife, Lauren, our K9 named Ben, and his handler, Joe. Our third visit would be a different type of investigation. Joe and Ben would work side by side with Virginia, and Lauren and I would quietly document the activity. Ben was a retired police K9 trained to work in unfamiliar locations on a daily basis, so Joe and I wanted to see if Ben could duplicate his job, except in a haunted location. Ben possessed various indicators for such things as where a person might be hiding or where drugs might be stashed — just a few examples of his abilities. Although we were not interested in looking for drugs, we could use Ben's human tracking training and other specific indicators. Even though we may not see a ghost, our hope was that Ben would, and then alert us to it. We saw amazing results during the first year that we utilized Ben. He seemed to react to events seconds before we experienced them. Sometimes Ben would even posture himself in a protective position between Joe and his team members and an unseen force. That was another indicator we would watch for. Ben was also a handler protection dog and would become extremely protective of the team as we were out working. It was comforting to know that he had our backs! On a humorous side note, during a few investigations Ben alerted Joe and the team that drugs were hidden in a few areas of our clients' homes. But those are stories for another time.

Our third investigation began earlier in the day. Virginia arrived and together we did another walk-through. Confident that no other entities occupied the home, Virginia now focused on the Hat Man's presence, which was predominantly in the basement. Once the walk-through was complete, Joe brought Ben in for a typical search, similar to what he would do on other jobs when searching for people. Ben is never leashed when searching, and as he moved through the living and dining rooms, he quickly ran down to the basement without command. This was significant considering Virginia's report that she felt the Hat Man strongest in that area. Following Ben's lead, we investigated with an EMF detector and audio recorder, but nothing significant was discovered. After a few minutes, Joe motioned Ben back up to the first floor and ran him through each room. Ben detected no humans or ghosts on the first floor, so we proceeded to the second floor and the attic area with no unusual indicators from Ben. After Ben's walk-through, we did a typical PPA condensed investigation throughout the house with Virginia, Lauren, Joe, Ben, and me, all working together as one team. All was relatively quiet with no flying quarters on this visit. Virginia's prior energy binding had more than likely diminished this activity. In one respect, we were thrilled that some of our strategies seemed to have an effect on the house. But on the other hand, as investigators, we are always excited to experience activity.

There came a point in the investigation where we decided to sit in the living room and just watch and listen. Nothing physical was happening so we wanted to see if just observing for a while would make a difference. And it did! As we were quietly sitting, Virginia turned towards the stairs and yelled, "There it goes, up the stairs!" Suddenly, Ben jumped up from a relaxed position. He bolted to the top of staircase without command, made a quick right turn then slammed into the wall, letting out a quick yelp. I asked Virginia, "What the hell just happened?" She explained that the Hat Man had come into the room and quickly darted up the stairs to the right. Ben is trained not to move without command, so totally ignoring his training left Joe stunned. Apparently, Ben did not realize he couldn't go through the wall with the energy! We checked on him, and he was fine! Unfortunately, Ben passed away a few years later. My time working with him and Joe was one of the best experiences of my paranormal career. Ben was more human than animal and we all became very emotionally attached to him. His death represented a great loss for the whole team, but we felt blessed to have known and worked with him!

Once we were satisfied with our inside work, Virginia was ready to tackle the Hat Man once more.

Since Gus would not try some of our recommendations, it became unlikely that the Hat Man would leave on his own. Virginia wanted to purge his presence from the house by binding him to the property. Part of this technique would occur inside the house and part outside in the backyard; the entire process would take over an hour. If we could not remove the entity from Gus completely, we were hopeful that we could at least keep it outside. Virginia bound the Hat Man to an area of earth in the backyard. With the ritual completed, we would now have to wait to see what the outcome would be. This would be our last visit to the Upper Darby home. Whether we were successful or not, there was nothing more we could safely do.

Choosy Ghosts Choose Jif, apparently! These jars were taken out of the pantry in the kitchen and found on the dining room table one afternoon.

Chapter 10

What Remains is Personal

Through my years of investigating the paranormal, I have learned when dealing with negative attachments, demons, or possessions, an interconnected relationship always exists with the victim. Energies are drawn together for a variety of reasons, and the connection is sometimes difficult to break. Part of our work strives to remove the foreign entity, but the other part has to be enacted by the victim to change the reason that the connection was made in the first place. That reason is not always apparent. Sometimes the victim may be consciously aware of the reason, such as someone summoning a demon for a specific purpose, but other times there can be a subconscious cause where the victim is unaware. Many times an attachment occurs because of sickness, drug use, alcohol abuse or another medical condition. Mental health issues can create an atmosphere for an attachment to occur, as well as being psychically open to allow someone from the other side to take note and jump in. Many times people receive attachments with no clue of their origin. Some people aren't even aware of attachments but recognize that their life is in turmoil. Whatever the cause, the conditions were right for two energies to align and connect, thus allowing the attachment to occur.

I have talked with many people who have broken the connection with an entity by simply adjusting their lifestyle to a much more positive way of living. Some people add prayer to their daily routines, other totally change their diets, and some work out and began having more fun. The key seems to be doing whatever it takes to raise a person's personal vibration to a point where the negative attachment is no longer compatible with the vibration of the victim. The victim, essentially, takes his or her power back. Victims of spiritual attack do not need an outside resource to help. They can cure their own issues. Of course this task can sometimes be extremely difficult and takes a vast amount of work and long-term commitment to change. But it can be done. Some people give up much too early without believing in themselves enough to make that change happen. Many resources are available to people enduring hauntings and attachments, but they need to screen them carefully and be certain that a legitimate team is chosen that can provide real help without making things worse. After everything else is cleared from a home, what remains with the victim is personal. Unless they are willing to put in the required time and effort, it may never go away.

Regarding our Upper Darby case, Gus was not willing to employ recommendations that could have severed the attachment. He had personal reasons, and we understood and respected those reasons. Virginia had subdued the Hat Man to a level much more tolerable than before, but we were still concerned about Gus moving forward. Even after Virginia's latest binding, unfortunately, Gus continued to have encounters with the Hat Man. It may have been because of the way it was sent to him or his belief in what it could do, but this was the most relentless spirit we have ever dealt with. Virginia's calling for divine guidance from the other side did not even prove helpful. This is usually indicative of situations that are in place for a victim's own spiritual growth and not meant to be solved by anyone else.

Months later, Virginia spoke with Sharan. The family had decided to move from the Upper Darby house. Virginia had previously encouraged them to leave if the activity persisted. This was the first time Virginia recommended moving to someone since we began working together. In this situation, Virginia strongly felt that Hat Man was bound to the property and if the family finally wanted the activity to end, they needed to move out of the house. Because property values were quickly dropping in the neighborhood, combined with their experiences in the home, they wanted a fresh start. This would be the big test to determine if Virginia's ritual had indeed bound the Hat Man to the property. After Sharan and Gus moved into their new home and spent a considerable amount of time there, we were extremely happy to hear that Gus had encountered no further activity and seemed to be free from this nightmare he had lived with for the past three years. Virginia's binding worked, and she hoped that the Hat Man would return to its origin now that Gus was gone.

Sharan, Gus, and their family have since left the state and moved south to pursue new career opportunities. They are happily living life with the Hat Man remaining only as a distant memory. Sharan later told us that on the day they moved out of Upper Darby, the house seemed to be reacting to their departure. Light bulbs popped, a hanging pendulum began swinging, and of course, a quarter was thrown at them.

May peace and happiness be with them in their new life!

Final Thoughts

I have been a parapsychologist for more than a decade where I have enjoyed the opportunity to study psychic ability and paranormal activity in many situations. When working with clients and spirits, alongside Psychic Medium Virginiarose Centrillo, we always view the situation in a holistic way. As I have stated several times in this book, an interconnected energy always exists between the living and the dead as they inhabit the same geographic space. In nearly every case, counseling must be used, emotionally, psychologically, or even socially, for both the living participants involved in a haunting or for the dearly departed who did not leave this earth for whatever reason. Whatever holds a ghost in an earth-bound existence must be identified and worked through before it moves to the next level of being. Additionally, hauntings affect humans in profound ways. A profusion of conditions may be causing stress for the witnesses, and many people have a hard time dealing with even a small amount of activity. We have also identified a host of ways in which the living contributes to the type of activity taking place. Just like people, ghosts either like or dislike individuals, based on how those people act and what they say. Ghosts will either get along with them, or they won't. It is then our job as a resolution team to identify any friction and try to remedy the cause.

Our team has also worked many negative attachment cases. While we have been successful in resolving most of them, I hold the belief that certain situations are just not meant to be resolved, perhaps because of a higher spiritual purpose that the victim may be working on, on another level. It is not our team's place to immediately solve every problem for every person. I believe some things happen for a reason, and we are often not meant to understand them on a human level. The Upper Darby poltergeist may have been one of those instances. Virginia often says that the house picks the people, not the other way around. Many people tell us that they just had a "feeling" about buying a particular house for whatever reason. Later, they found it was haunted. It may be that we, and people who die before us, become aligned with the universe on some higher level and are mutually guided through certain events together so we can encounter new experiences, good or bad. The Upper Darby house brought seven of our team members together with seven members of a family. Three other people joined us, and we mutually experienced something that very few get the chance to experience. Although Sharan, Gus, and their family bore the brunt of the activity, they reached out for help and included us in their journey. Looking back more than nine years later, my team and I learned so much from the haunting and our interaction with Gus and Sharan. Our team has evolved greatly since then, adding many additional resources and growing in wisdom. Should Sharan have contacted the PPA today, we likely would have been more successful in helping them initially.

Virginia will support me when I say that I cringe any time she suggests that a person should move from a property. Moving is difficult, financially hard, disruptive, and time consuming. Frankly speaking, my ego also takes a hit when we are not able to completely solve a problem for someone. However, Virginia is also correct when she says that many people find themselves in a far worse situation by staying where they are. Sometimes we often work on hauntings where someone in the house is a psychic medium, even if they don't realize it. They may live in negative neighborhoods, which can be detrimental. Even if we removed every ghost from a medium's house, it is likely that they would pick something up psychically from somewhere else in the neighborhood. Psychically open people can also pick up old energy empathetically, which in turn can cause all types of physical or emotional issues.

In the case of Upper Darby, I think moving was right for Gus and Sharan. Sharan was very open, as were her children, and this would have made living there for a long period of time difficult. Virginia felt that since their street was so active with earthbound spirits, sooner or later, someone in the house would have brought a wandering spirit home with them. Gus was struggling to understand everything because he more or less didn't believe in ghosts. The ghosts, consequently, seemed to be changing his mind. Obviously, having an attachment was a frightening issue, and moving off the property was the final step in detaching the entity once and for all.

I cannot say for certain that every single event in the home was caused by a ghost, but I can say that the amount of activity caused by a ghost was enough to drive a person crazy. Many other families have fallen apart because of stress in dealing with this type of activity day after day, but this family held it together. Much credit goes to Gus, Sharan, and their family for pushing through. Hopefully, their experiences will someday be helpful to others enduring similar situations.

As for me, this family is often in my thoughts and their story is one I frequently talk about. During radio interviews and public lectures, I often get asked the question, "What is the craziest thing you ever experienced on a case?" The answer is always the same — The Upper Darby Poltergeist!

Further Information

Much of the evidence documented during this investigation has been added to the Pennsylvania Paranormal Association website and is available for review.

Go to **www.theppa.net** and click on the **CASE FILES** link at the top of the page.

Scroll down to **Delaware County** and click on **File No. 10-11-047** and **File No. 11-06-72**.

CPSIA information can be obtained
at www.ICGtesting.com
Printed in the USA
BVHW080906180719
553798BV00002B/272/P

9 781644 460078